Beat distraction
to make time for
your Highlight

Adjust and
...our
...ry day

LASER   REFLECT

ENERGIZE

Take care of your body
to recharge your brain

MAKE TIME

MAKE TIME

HOW TO FOCUS ON WHAT MATTERS EVERY DAY

JAKE KNAPP AND
JOHN ZERATSKY

CURRENCY
NEW YORK

Copyright © 2018 by John Knapp and John Zeratsky

Published in the United States by Currency,
an imprint of the Crown Publishing Group,
a division of Penguin Random House LLC, New York.
crownpublishing.com

CURRENCY and its colophon are trademarks of Penguin Random House LLC.

Currency books are available at special discounts for bulk purchases for sales promotions or corporate use. Special editions, including personalized covers, excerpts of existing books, or books with corporate logos, can be created in large quantities for special needs. For more information, contact Premium Sales at (212) 572-2232 or e-mail specialmarkets@penguinrandomhouse.com.

Library of Congress Cataloging-in-Publication Data
Names: Knapp, Jake, author. | Zeratsky, John (Product designer), author.
Title: Make time : how to focus on what matters every day.
Description: New York : Currency, [2018] | Includes bibliographical references and index.
Identifiers: LCCN 2017059817 | ISBN 9780525572428
Subjects: LCSH: Time management. | Work-life balance. | Self-realization.
Classification: LCC BF637.T5 K63 2018 | DDC 650.1/1—dc23
LC record available at https://lccn.loc.gov/2017059817

ISBN 978-0-525-57242-8
Ebook ISBN 978-0-525-57243-5

Printed in the United States of America

Book design by Andrea Lau
Illustrations by Jake Knapp (with Luke Knapp and Flynn Knapp)
Jacket design by Zak Tebbal
Jacket photograph: (iPhone) Rafael Fernandez/Wikimedia Commons

10 9 8 7 6 5 4 3 2 1

First Edition

For Holly and MICHELLE

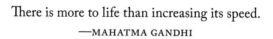

There is more to life than increasing its speed.

—MAHATMA GANDHI

CONTENTS

HIGHLIGHT

Highlight Tactics

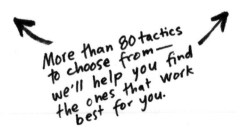

More than 80 tactics to choose from — we'll help you find the ones that work best for you.

LASER

Laser Tactics

ENERGIZE

Energize Tactics

Reflect 237

Start "Someday" Today 247

MAKE
TIME

INTRODUCTION

This is how people talk nowadays:

And this is how our calendars look:

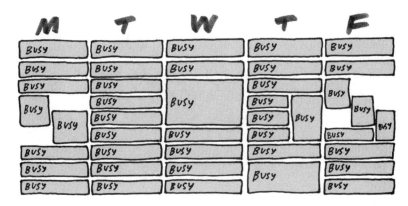

All day, our phones never stop:

And by evening, we're almost too tired for Netflix:

Do you ever look back and wonder "What did I really *do* today?" Do you ever daydream about projects and activities you'll get to someday—but "someday" never comes?

This is a book about slowing down the crazy rush. It's about making time for things that matter. We believe it's possible to feel less busy, be less distracted, and enjoy the present moment more. Maybe that sounds a little hippy-dippy, but we're serious.

Make Time is not about productivity. It's not about getting more done, finishing your to-dos faster, or outsourcing your life. Instead, it's a framework designed to help you actually *create more time in your day* for the things you care about, whether that's spending time with your family, learning a language, starting a side business, volunteering, writing a novel, or mastering Mario Kart. Whatever you want time for, we think Make Time can help you get it. Moment by moment and day by day, you can make your life your own.

We want to start by talking about *why* life is so busy and chaotic these days. And why, if you feel constantly stressed and distracted, it's probably not your fault.

In the twenty-first century, two very powerful forces compete for every minute of your time. The first is what we call the Busy Bandwagon. The Busy Bandwagon is our culture of constant busyness—

the overflowing inboxes, stuffed calendars, and endless to-do lists. According to the Busy Bandwagon mindset, if you want to meet the demands of the modern workplace and function in modern society, you must fill every minute with productivity. After all, everyone else is busy. If you slow down, you'll fall behind and never catch up.

The second force competing for your time is what we call the Infinity Pools. Infinity Pools are apps and other sources of endlessly replenishing content. If you can pull to refresh, it's an Infinity Pool. If it streams, it's an Infinity Pool. This always-available, always-new entertainment is your reward for the exhaustion of constant busyness.

But is constant busyness *really* mandatory? Is endless distraction *really* a reward? Or are we all just stuck on autopilot?

Most of Our Time Is Spent by Default

Both forces—the Busy Bandwagon and the Infinity Pools—are powerful because they've become our *defaults*. In technology lingo, *default* means the way something works when you first start using it. It's a preselected option, and if you don't do something to change it, that default is what you get. For example, if you buy a new phone, by default you get email and Web browser apps on the homescreen. By default, you get a notification for every new message. The phone has a default wallpaper image and a default ring tone. All these options have been preselected by Apple or Google or whoever made your phone; you can change the settings if you want to, but it takes work, so many defaults just stick.

There are defaults in nearly every part of our lives. It's not just our devices; our workplaces and our culture have built-in defaults that make busy and distracted the normal, typical state of affairs. These standard settings are *everywhere*. Nobody ever looked at an empty calendar and said, "The best way to spend this time is to cram it full of random meetings!" Nobody ever said, "The most important thing today is everybody else's whims!" Of course not. That would be crazy. But because of defaults, it's exactly what we do. In the office, every meeting defaults to thirty or sixty minutes even if the business at hand actually requires only a quick chat. By default other people choose what goes on our calendars, and by default we're expected to be okay with back-to-back-to-back meetings. The rest of our work defaults to email and messaging systems, and by default we check our inboxes constantly and reply-all immediately.

React to what's in front of you. Be responsive. Fill your time, be efficient, and get more done. These are the default rules of the Busy Bandwagon.

When we tear ourselves away from the Busy Bandwagon, the Infinity Pools are ready to lure us in. While the Busy Bandwagon defaults to endless tasks, the Infinity Pools default to endless distraction. Our phones, laptops, and televisions are filled with games, social feeds, and videos. Everything is at our fingertips, irresistible, even addictive. Every bump of friction is smoothed away.

Refresh Facebook. Browse YouTube. Keep up on the nonstop breaking news, play Candy Crush, binge-watch HBO. These are the defaults behind the ravenous Infinity Pools, devouring every scrap of time the Busy Bandwagon leaves behind. With the average person spending four-plus hours a day on their smartphone and another four-plus hours watching TV shows, distraction is quite literally a full-time job.

There you are in the middle, pulled in opposite directions by the Busy Bandwagon and the Infinity Pools. But what about *you*? What do you want from your days and from your life? What would happen if you could override these defaults and create your own?

Willpower isn't the way out. We've tried to resist the siren song of these forces ourselves, and we know how impossible it can be. We also spent years working in the technology industry, and we understand these apps, games, and devices well enough to know that they eventually will wear you down.

Productivity isn't the solution, either. We've tried to shave time off chores and cram in more to-dos. The trouble is, there are always more tasks and requests waiting to take their place. The faster you run on the hamster wheel, the faster it spins.

But there *is* a way to free your attention from those competing distractions and take back control of your time. That's where this book comes in. Make Time is a framework for choosing what you want to focus on, building the energy to do it, and breaking the default cycle so that you can start being more intentional about the way you live your life. Even if you don't completely control your own schedule—and few of us do—you absolutely can control your attention.

We want to help you set your own defaults. With new habits and new mindsets, you can stop reacting to the modern world and start actively making time for the people and activities that matter to you. This isn't about saving time. It's about *making* time for what matters.

The ideas in this book can give you space in your calendar, in your brain, and in your days. That space can bring clarity and calm to everyday life. It can create opportunities to start new hobbies or get to that "someday" project. A little space in your life might even unlock creative energy you lost or never found in the first place. But before we get into all of that, we'd like to explain who the heck we are, why we're so obsessed with time and energy, and how we came up with Make Time.

Meet the Time Dorks

We are Jake and JZ.[1] We are not rocket-building billionaires like Elon Musk, handsome Renaissance men like Tim Ferriss, or genius executives like Sheryl Sandberg. Most time-management advice is written by or about superhumans, but you will find no superhumanity in these pages. We're normal, fallible human beings who get stressed out and distracted just like everyone else.

What makes our perspective unusual is that we're product designers who spent years in the tech industry helping to build services like

---

1 In this book, "JZ" stands for John Zeratsky. Not to be confused with the musician and business mogul Jay-Z. Try not to be disappointed.

Gmail, YouTube, and Google Hangouts. As designers, our job was to turn abstract ideas (like "Wouldn't it be cool if email sorted itself?") into real-life solutions (like Gmail's Priority Inbox). We had to understand how technology fits into—and changes—daily life. This experience gives us insight into why Infinity Pools are so compelling, and how to prevent them from taking over.

A few years ago, we realized we could apply design to something invisible: how we spent our time. But instead of starting with a technology or business opportunity, we started with the most meaningful projects and the most important people in our lives.

Each day, we tried to make a little time for our own personal top priority. We questioned the defaults of the Busy Bandwagon and redesigned our to-do lists and calendars. We questioned the defaults of the Infinity Pools and redesigned how and when we used technology. We don't have limitless willpower, so every redesign had to be easy to use. We couldn't erase every obligation, so we worked with constraints. We experimented, failed, and succeeded, and, over time, we learned.

In this book, we'll share the principles and tactics we've discovered, along with many tales of our human errors and dorky solutions. We thought this one was a good place to start:

 The Backstory, Part 1: The Distraction-Free iPhone

Jake

It was 2012, and my two sons were playing with a wooden train in our living room. Luke (age: eight) was diligently assembling the track while Flynn (age: baby) drooled on a locomotive. Then Luke picked his head up and said:

MAKE TIME

His question wasn't intended to make me feel bad; he was just curious. But I didn't have a good answer. I mean, sure, there was probably *some* excuse for checking my email right at that moment. But not a great one. All day, I'd been looking forward to spending time with my kids, and now that it was finally happening, I wasn't really there at all.

At that moment, something clicked. It wasn't just that I had succumbed to one moment of distraction—I had a bigger problem.

Every day, I realized, I was *reacting:* to my calendar, to incoming email, to the infinite stream of new stuff on the Internet. Moments with my family were slipping past me, and for what? So I could answer one more message or check off another to-do?

The realization was frustrating because I was already trying to find balance. When Luke was born in 2003, I'd set out on a mission to become more productive at work so that I could spend more quality time at home.

By 2012, I considered myself a master of productivity and efficiency. I kept reasonable hours and was home in time for dinner every night. This was what work/life balance looked like, or so I believed.

But if that was the case, why was my eight-year-old son calling me out for being distracted? If I was so on top of things at work, why did I always feel so busy and scattered? If I started the morning with two hundred emails and got to zero by midnight, was that really a successful day?

Then it hit me: Being more productive didn't mean I was doing the most important work; it only meant I was reacting to other people's priorities faster.

As a result of being constantly online, I wasn't present enough with my children. And I was perpetually putting off my big "someday" goal of writing a book. In fact, I'd procrastinated for years without typing so much as a page. I'd been too busy treading water in a sea of other people's emails, other people's status updates, and snapshots of other people's lunch.

I wasn't just disappointed in myself, I was pissed off. In a fit of irritation, I grabbed my phone and furiously uninstalled Twitter, Facebook, and Instagram. As each icon disappeared from my homescreen, I felt a weight lift.

Then I stared at the Gmail app and gritted my teeth. At that time, I had a job at Google, and I'd spent years working on the Gmail team. I loved Gmail. But I knew what I had to do. I can still remember the message that popped up on the screen asking me, almost in disbelief, if I was sure I wanted to remove the app. I swallowed hard and tapped "Delete."

Without my apps, I expected to feel anxiety and isolation. And in the days after that, I *did* notice a change. But I wasn't stressed; instead, I felt relief. I felt free.

I stopped reflexively reaching for my iPhone at the slightest hint of boredom. Time with my kids slowed down in a good way. "Holy smokes," I thought. "If the iPhone wasn't making me happier, what about everything else?"

I loved my iPhone and all the futuristic powers it gave me. But I also had accepted every default that came with those powers, leaving me constantly tethered to the shiny device in my pocket. I started wondering how many other parts of my life needed to be reexamined, reset, and redesigned. What other defaults was I accepting blindly, and how could I take charge?

Soon after my iPhone experiment I took a new job. It was still at Google, only now I worked at Google Ventures, a venture-capital firm that invested money in outside startups.

The first day there, I met a guy named John Zeratsky.

At first, I wanted to dislike him. John is younger and—let's be honest—better-looking than I am. Even more despicable, however, was his constant calm. John was never stressed. He completed important work ahead of schedule yet somehow found time for side projects. He woke early, finished work early, went home early. He was always smiling. What the hell was his deal?

Well, I ended up getting along just fine with John, or as I call him, JZ. I soon discovered he was a kindred spirit—my brother from another mother, if you will.

Like me, JZ was disillusioned with the Busy Bandwagon. We both loved technology and had spent years designing tech services (while I was at Gmail, he was at YouTube). But we were both beginning to understand the cost of these Infinity Pools to our attention and time.

And like me, JZ was on a mission to do something about it. He was kind of like Obi-Wan Kenobi about this stuff, only instead of a robe, he wore plaid shirts and jeans, and instead of the Force, he was interested in what he called "the system." It was almost mystical. He didn't know exactly what it was, but he believed it existed: a simple framework for avoiding distractions, maintaining energy, and making more time.

I know; it sounded kind of weird to me, too. But the more he talked about what such a system could look like, the more I found myself nodding my head. JZ was *way* into ancient human history and evolutionary psychology, and he saw that part of the problem was rooted in the huge disconnect between our hunter-gatherer roots and our crazy modern world. He looked through the lens of a product designer and figured this "system" would work only if it changed our defaults, making distractions harder to access instead of relying on willpower to constantly fight them.

Well, heck, I thought. If we *could* create this system, it would be exactly what I was looking for. So I teamed up with JZ, and the quest began.

The Backstory, Part 2: Our Dorky Quest to Make Time

JZ

Jake's distraction-free iPhone was a bit extreme, and I admit I didn't try it right away. But once I did, I loved it. So the two of us began searching for other redesigns—ways to switch our default setting from "distracted" to "focused."

I started reading the news only once a week and reprogrammed my sleep schedule to become a morning person. I experimented with eating six small meals a day and then tried eating just two large ones. I adopted different exercise regimens, from distance running to yoga classes to daily push-ups. I even persuaded my programmer friends to build me customized to-do-list apps. Meanwhile, Jake spent a full year tracking his daily energy levels in a spreadsheet, trying to understand whether he should drink coffee or green tea, whether he should exercise in the morning or the evening, and even whether he liked being around people (the answer: yes . . . mostly).

We learned a lot from this obsessive behavior, but we were interested in more than just what worked for *us;* we still believed in the idea of a system that anyone could tailor to their own life. To find it, we'd need some human test subjects besides ourselves, and as luck would have it, we had the perfect laboratory.

While working at Google, Jake created something he called a "design sprint": basically a workweek redesigned from the ground up. For five days, a team would cancel all meetings and focus on solving a single problem, following a specific checklist of activities. It was our first effort at designing *time* rather than products, and it worked—the design sprint quickly spread across Google.

In 2012, we started working together to run design sprints with startups in the Google Ventures portfolio. Over the next few years, we ran more than 150 of these five-day sprints. Nearly a thousand people participated: programmers, nutritionists, CEOs, baristas, farmers, and more.

For a couple of Time Dorks, the whole thing was an amazing opportunity. We had the chance to redesign the workweek and learn from hundreds of high-performing teams at startups including Slack, Uber, and 23andMe. Many of the principles behind Make Time were inspired by what we discovered in those sprints.

Four Lessons from the Design Sprint Laboratory

The first thing we learned was that **something magic happens when you start the day with one high-priority goal.** Each sprint day, we drew attention to one big focal point: On Monday, the team creates a map of the problem; on Tuesday, each person sketches one solution; on Wednesday, they decide which solutions are best; on Thursday, they build a prototype; and on Friday, they test it. Each day's goal is ambitious, but it's just one thing.

This focal point creates clarity and motivation. When you have one ambitious but achievable goal, at the end of the day, you're *done*. You can check it off, let go of work, and go home satisfied.

Another lesson from our design sprints was that **we got more done**

when we banned devices. Since we set the rules, we were able to prohibit laptops and smartphones, and the difference was phenomenal. Without the constant lure of email and other Infinity Pools, people brought their complete attention to the task at hand, and the default switched to focus.

We also learned about **the importance of energy for focused work and clear thinking.** When we first started running design sprints, teams worked long hours, fueled by sugary treats. Late in the week, energy would plummet. So we made adjustments, and saw how things like a healthy lunch, a quick walk, frequent breaks, and a slightly shorter workday helped maintain peak energy, resulting in better and more effective work.

Lastly, these experiments taught us the power of, well, experiments. **Experimenting allowed us to improve the process,** and seeing the results of our changes firsthand gave us a deep confidence that we never could have built just by reading about someone else's results.

Our sprints required a whole team and a whole week, but we could see right away that there was no reason individuals couldn't redesign their days in a similar way. The lessons we learned became the foundation for Make Time.

Of course, it wasn't a yellow brick road to perfection. We still got swept up in the Busy Bandwagon and sucked into the Infinity Pools of distraction now and again. Although some of our tactics turned into habits, others sputtered and failed. But taking stock of our results each day helped us understand *why* we tripped up. And this experimental approach also allowed us to be kinder to ourselves when we made mistakes—after all, every mistake was just a data point, and we could always try again tomorrow.

Despite our stumbles, Make Time was resilient. We found ourselves with more energy and headspace than we'd ever had, and we were able to take on bigger projects: the kinds of "someday" things we'd never been able to get around to before.

Jake

I wanted to start writing in the evenings, but realized that the lure of watching TV was a big problem. So I experimented and made a serious change to my defaults, putting the DVD player in the closet and unsubscribing from Netflix. With the freed-up time, I started working on an adventure novel, and I stuck with it, pausing only when we wrote our book *Sprint*. Writing was something I'd wanted to do since I was a kid, and making time for it felt awesome.

JZ

For years, my wife, Michelle, and I had dreamed of taking long sailing trips together. So we bought an old sailboat and started spending our weekends fixing it up. We applied the same tactic of choosing one daily task and putting time on the calendar to get it done and as a result made time to learn about diesel engine maintenance, electricity, and ocean navigation. Together we've now sailed from San Francisco to Southern California, Mexico, and beyond.

We were so excited about our results that we started blogging about the Make Time techniques that worked for us. Hundreds of thousands of people read the posts, and many of those readers wrote to us. Of course, some of them wanted to inform us that we're self-righteous morons, but the vast majority of responses were inspiring and awesome. People experienced dramatic changes from tactics such as removing apps on their smartphones and prioritizing one task each day. They found renewed energy and felt happier. The experiments worked for lots of people, not just for us! As one reader told us, "It's weird how easy the switch was."

And that's just it: Reclaiming your time and attention can be weirdly easy. As Jake learned from his distraction-free iPhone, the changes do not require tons of self-discipline. Instead, change comes from resetting defaults, creating barriers, and beginning to design the way you spend your time. Once you start using Make Time, these small positive shifts become self-reinforcing. The more you try it, the more you'll learn about yourself and the more the system will improve.

Make Time isn't anti-technology; we're both tech nerds, after all. We won't ask you to disconnect entirely or become a hermit. You can still follow your friends on Instagram, read the news, and send emails like a modern person. But by challenging the standard behaviors in our efficiency-obsessed, distraction-saturated world, you can get the best of technology *and* put yourself back in control. And once you take control, you can change the game.

HOW MAKE TIME WORKS

Make Time Is Just Four Steps, Repeated Every Day

The four daily steps of Make Time are inspired by what we learned from design sprints, from our own experiments, and from readers who have tried out the framework and shared their results. Here's a zoomed-out view of how each day looks:

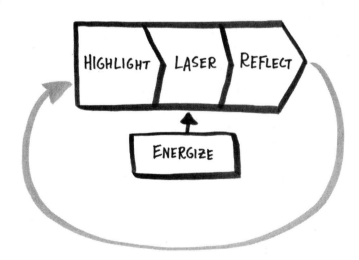

The first step is choosing a single **highlight** to prioritize in your day. Next, you'll employ specific tactics to stay **laser-focused** on that highlight—we'll offer a menu of tricks to beat distraction in an always-connected world. Throughout the day, you'll build **energy** so you can stay in control of your time and attention. Finally, you'll **reflect** on the day with a few simple notes.

Let's zoom in for a closer look at those four steps.

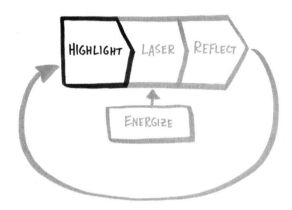

Highlight: Start Each Day by Choosing a Focal Point

The first step in Make Time is deciding what you want to make time *for*. Every day, you'll choose **a single activity to prioritize and protect in your calendar.** It might be an important goal at work, like finishing a presentation. You might choose something at home, like cooking dinner or planting your garden. Your Highlight might be something you don't necessarily *have* to do but *want* to do, like playing with your kids or reading a book. Your Highlight can contain multiple steps; for example, finishing that presentation might include writing the closing remarks, completing the slides, and doing a practice run-through. By setting "finish presentation" as your Highlight, you commit to complete all the tasks required.

Of course, your Highlight isn't the only thing you'll do each day.

But it will be your priority. Asking yourself "What's going to be the highlight of my day?" ensures that you spend time on the things that matter to *you* and don't lose the entire day reacting to other people's priorities. When you choose a Highlight, you put yourself in a positive, proactive frame of mind.

To help you do that, we'll share our favorite tactics for choosing a daily Highlight and actually making time to accomplish it. But this alone isn't enough. You'll also need to rethink how you react to distractions that might get in your way, and that's exactly what the next step is all about.

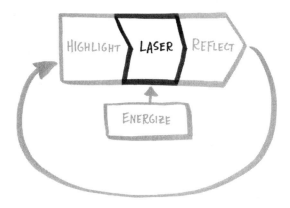

Laser: Beat Distraction to Make Time for Your Highlight

Distractions like email, social media, and breaking news are everywhere, and they're not going away. You can't go live in a cave, throw away your gadgets, and swear off technology entirely. But you can re-design the way you *use* technology to stop the reaction cycle.

We'll show you how to **adjust your technology so you can find Laser mode.** Simple changes like logging out of social media apps or scheduling time to check email can have a huge effect—we'll provide specific tactics to help you focus.

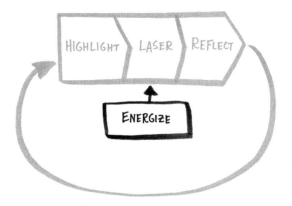

Energize: Use the Body to Recharge the Brain

To achieve focus and make time for what matters, your brain needs energy, and that energy comes from taking care of your body.

That's why the third component of Make Time is to **charge your battery with exercise, food, sleep, quiet, and face-to-face time.** It's not as hard as it might sound. The lifestyle defaults of the twenty-first century ignore our evolutionary history and rob us of energy. That's actually good news: Because things are so out of whack, there are a lot of easy fixes.

The Energize section contains many tactics you can choose from, including sneaking a nap, giving yourself partial credit for exercise, and learning how to use caffeine strategically. We won't ask you to become a fitness freak or adopt a wacky diet. Instead, we'll offer simple shifts you can make for the immediate reward of having energy for the things you want to do.

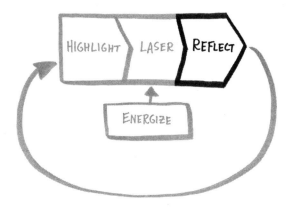

Reflect: Adjust and Improve Your System

Finally, before going to bed, you'll **take a few notes**. It's super simple: You'll decide which tactics you want to continue and which ones you want to refine or drop.[2] And you'll think back on your energy level, whether you made time for your Highlight, and what brought you joy in the day.

Over time, you'll build a customized daily system tailored to your unique habits and routines, your unique brain and body, and your unique goals and priorities.

The Make Time Tactics: Pick, Test, Repeat

This book includes dozens of tactics for putting Make Time into practice. Some tactics will work for you, but some won't (and some may just sound nuts). It's like a cookbook. You wouldn't try all the recipes at once, and you don't need to do all the tactics at once, either.

Instead, you'll pick, test, and repeat. As you read, take note of any tactics you want to try. Fold the corner of the page or make a

---

2   Or, in the immortal words of Rob Base and DJ Easy Rock: "Take it off the rack, if it's wack, put it back."

list on a piece of paper. Look for tactics that seem doable but a little challenging—and especially, look for tactics that sound like fun.

On your first day using Make Time, we suggest trying one tactic from each step. That is, one new tactic to help you make time for your Highlight, one that keeps you laser-focused by changing how you react to distractions, and one for building energy—three tactics total.

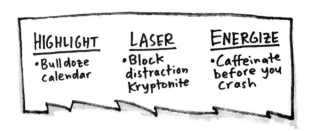

HIGHLIGHT
• Bulldoze calendar

LASER
• Block distraction Kryptonite

ENERGIZE
• Caffeinate before you crash

You don't necessarily have to try something new every day. If what you're doing is working, keep it up! But if it isn't or if you think it could work better still, each day is a chance to experiment. Your version of the Make Time system will be totally personalized, and because you built it yourself, you'll trust it, and it will fit into your existing lifestyle.

No Perfection Required

While developing Make Time, we immersed ourselves in books, blogs, magazines, and scientific research. A lot of what we read was intimidating. We were confronted with hundreds of glossy, perfect lives: the effortlessly organized executive, the enlightened mindful yogi, the writer with the perfect process, the carefree host pan-searing trumpet mushrooms with one hand while blowtorching crème brûlées with the other.

It's stressful, isn't it? None of us can be perfect eaters, perfectly productive, perfectly mindful, and perfectly rested all the time. We can't do the fifty-seven things bloggers tell us we're supposed to do before 5 a.m. And even if we could, we *shouldn't*. Perfection is a distraction—another shiny object taking your attention away from your real priorities.

We'd like you to forget the idea of perfection when it comes to Make Time. Don't even try to do it perfectly—there's no such thing! But there's also no way to screw it up. And you won't have to start over if you "fall off the wagon," because each day is a clean slate.

Keep in mind that neither of us uses all the tactics in this book all the time. We use some tactics all the time and some tactics some of the time, and we each use some tactics *none* of the time. There are things that work for JZ that do not work for Jake and vice versa. We each have our own imperfect formula, and that formula can change depending on what's going on. When Jake is traveling, he temporarily installs an email app on his phone, and JZ has been known to binge-watch Netflix on occasion—*Stranger Things* is so good! The goal is not monastic vows but a workable and flexible set of habits.

The "Everyday" Mindset

If you read Make Time cover to cover, it can feel like a lot to do. Heck, even if you skip around the book—which we encourage—it can still feel like a lot to do. So instead of thinking of these tactics as "more things you have to do," consider ways to make them part of your normal life. That's why we suggest, for example, walking to work (page 181) and exercising at home (page 184) rather than an expensive gym membership or an hourlong fitness class every morning.

The best tactics are the ones that fit into your day. They're not something you force yourself to do; they're just something you do. And in most cases, they'll be things you *want* to do.

We're confident Make Time will help you create space in your life for the things that matter most. And once you start, you'll find that Make Time is self-reinforcing. You can begin with one small change. Positive results will compound as you go and you'll be able to tackle bigger and bigger goals. Even if you're already a master of efficiency, you can use Make Time to bring attention and satisfaction to what's working well.

We can't get you out of every pointless meeting or magically set your inbox to zero, and we won't try to turn you into a Zen master. But we can help you slow down a little, turn down the noise of the modern world, and find more joy in each day.

Highlight

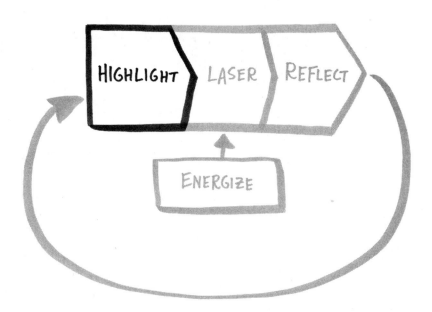

We do not remember days,
we remember moments.

—CESARE PAVESE

If you want to make time for things that matter, the Busy Bandwagon will tell you the answer is to do *more*. Get more done. Be more efficient. Set more goals and make more plans. It's the only way to fit those important moments into your life.

We disagree. Doing more doesn't help you create time for what matters; it just makes you feel even more frazzled and busy. And when you're busy day after day, time slides by in a blur.

This chapter is about stopping the blur, slowing down, and actually experiencing the moments you want to savor and remember rather than rushing through them just to get to that next item on your to-do list. This idea is pretty simple, but we came about it the hard way, by losing weeks and months of our own lives to a whirling churn of busyness.

The Missing Months

JZ

It was early 2008, the beginning of one of the snowiest winters in Chicago's history. The days were short. The streets were a mess. Getting to work was a daily battle against the elements. And one day I woke up with a shocking realization: I couldn't remember the last two months.

Don't be alarmed. I didn't have any scary medical problems, and I wasn't unwittingly tangled in a Jason Bourne–style CIA plot. But it was still serious. The months had simply disappeared, without texture or terrain or footprints to mark their passage.

And I *wanted* to remember that time, because things were going well. I had a good job, a great girlfriend, and close friends who lived nearby. An outsider would have looked at my life and said, "He's living the dream." So why did I feel disconnected from the reality of my dreamlike life?

I didn't know what was wrong, but I sure did want to figure it out. So, naturally, I began experimenting.

I started by getting productive. I thought if I packed more into each day, I'd have more to remember. A couple of years earlier, while working at a fast-paced tech startup, I became obsessed with making the most of every hour. My work was neatly planned and organized; I processed and cleared my inbox every day; I even carried a stack of notecards in my pocket so I could capture any spontaneous thoughts or ideas. Not a single moment of thinking time was to be wasted!

That worked well enough at the office, so I wondered:

Could these kinds of productivity hacks help me make the most of my time at home, too? I began to see my life as a problem to be solved with categorized to-do lists, a rigid calendar, and an absurd filing system.

It didn't work. I was so focused on small tasks that the days slipped by even faster than before. The blur was getting worse. It sucked.

I decided to overhaul my approach. Instead of obsessively managing my minutes, I turned my attention to the long term. I created lists of one-year, three-year, five-year, and ten-year goals, which I asked my girlfriend to review and discuss with me. (The next year she married me, so I guess she was on the same page with at least *one* of my goals.)

Setting goals seemed more meaningful than optimizing my to-do list, but I still felt adrift—these objectives were too far away to be motivating. And there were other problems: What if my priorities changed? All of a sudden I'd realize I was working toward a goal that no longer mattered to me. And living a "someday" life was demoralizing. In the words of author James Clear, I was essentially saying, "I'm not good enough yet, but I will be when I reach my goal."

My experiments weren't working. I was stuck between day-to-day minutiae and too-far-away goals, and the dreary February and March weather did nothing to lift my spirits. But eventually, the winter ended, spring turned to summer, the birds started to sing, and almost by accident, I began to see the solution I'd been looking for.

I realized I didn't need perfectly planned task lists or well-crafted long-term plans. Instead, it was simple but satisfying activities that helped stop the blurring of time. For example, I started meeting a group of friends every Friday for lunch at a restaurant across town. I would look forward to that all week. Other days, I'd go for a run along the lakefront after work. And when the weather was right, I'd sometimes leave the office early, walk to the harbor, and go sailing for a few hours before sunset. The long days and warm nights sure helped—summer arrived at exactly the right time for me that year. I had been lucky to stumble upon a way to add meaning to each day and fortunate to recognize it as the solution to my problem.

It wasn't just outside-the-office plans that helped me stop the blur. After seeing how much making time for those activities helped, I began to think of my work in terms of more meaningful activities, too. Instead of checking off as many to-dos as possible or racing to clear my inbox before heading home, I focused on accomplishments that were satisfying and important. One day I found myself looking forward to a big presentation I was giving to executives, and I realized it was similar to the satisfaction I got from the lunches, lakefront jogs, and evening sails. I started thinking less about my to-do list and more about substantial projects like leading design workshops and spending a day fixing software bugs with engineers.

Of course, my life wasn't all social lunches and milestones at work. I had plenty of mundane stuff to get done, like answering emails, keeping our apartment clean, and returning library books before the deadline. And I *did* get those things done, but they weren't where I directed my greatest focus.

As I reflected on my missing months and what helped me stop the blur of time, I began to understand something: I loved thinking about big, lofty goals and I was good at getting things done hour by hour, but neither was truly satisfying. I was happiest when I had something I could hold on to in the present—a chunk of time that was bigger than a to-do but smaller than a five-year goal. An activity I could plan for, look forward to, and appreciate when it was done.

In other words, I needed to make sure every day had a highlight.

We believe that focusing on these in-between activities—in the space between goals and tasks—is the key to slowing down, bringing satisfaction to your daily life, and helping you make time. Long-term goals are useful for orienting you in the right direction but make it hard to enjoy the time spent working along the way. And tasks are necessary to get things done, but without a focal point, they fly by in a forgettable haze.

TASKS
Too machine-like

HIGH-LIGHT
Just right

GOALS
Too far away

Plenty of self-help gurus have offered suggestions for setting goals and plenty of productivity experts have created systems for getting things done, but the space between has been neglected. We call the missing piece a Highlight.

What Will Be the Highlight of Your Day?

We want you to begin each day by thinking about what you hope will be the bright spot. If, at the end of the day, someone asks you, "What was the highlight of your day?" what do you want your answer to be? When you look back on your day, what activity or accomplishment or moment do you want to savor? That's your Highlight.

Your Highlight is not the only thing you'll do each day. After all, most of us can't ignore our inboxes or say no to our bosses. But choosing a Highlight gives you a chance to be proactive about how you spend your time instead of letting technology, office defaults, and other people set your agenda. And although the Busy Bandwagon says you should try to be as productive as possible each day, we know it's better to focus on your priorities even if that means you don't get to everything on your to-do list.

Your Highlight gives each day a focal point. Research shows that the way you experience your days is not determined primarily by what happens *to you*. In fact, you create your own reality by choosing what *you pay attention to*.[1] This might seem obvious, but we think it's a big deal: You can design your time by choosing where you direct your attention. And your daily Highlight is the target of that attention.

Focusing on a daily Highlight stops the tug-of-war between Infinity Pool distractions and the demands of the Busy Bandwagon. It reveals a third path: being intentional and focused about how you spend your time.

Three Ways to Pick Your Highlight

Choosing your daily Highlight starts with asking yourself a question:

What do I want to be the highlight of my day?

Answering this question isn't always easy, especially when you're just beginning to use Make Time. Sometimes you've got many important tasks. Maybe there's one you're super excited about ("Bake birthday cake"), one with a looming deadline ("Finish slide deck"), or even a nasty job hanging over your head ("Put rat traps in garage").

So how should you decide? We use three different criteria to choose our Highlight.

---

1   For a fascinating summary of this research and how it applies to work and life, check out *Rapt* by Winifred Gallagher. It's one of JZ's favorite books.

Urgency

The first strategy is all about urgency: **What's the most pressing thing I have to do today?**

Have you ever spent hours churning through email and attending meetings only to realize at the end of the day that you failed to make time for the one thing you *really* needed to do? Well, we have. Lots of times. And whenever it happens, we feel miserable. Oh, the regret!

If you have something that absolutely positively *must* be accomplished today, make it your Highlight. You often can find urgent Highlights on your to-do list, email, or calendar—look for projects that are time-sensitive, important, and medium-size (in other words, they don't take ten minutes but don't take ten hours, either).

Your urgent Highlight might be one of the following:

- Create a price quote and send it to a customer who's expecting it before the end of the week.
- Request catering and venue proposals for an event you're organizing at work.
- Prepare and cook dinner before friends come over.
- Help your daughter finish a big school project that's due tomorrow.
- Edit and share vacation photos that your family is eager to see.

Satisfaction

The second Highlight strategy is to think about satisfaction: **At the end of the day, which Highlight will bring me the most satisfaction?**

Whereas the first strategy is all about what *needs* to get done, this strategy encourages you to focus on what you *want* to get done.

Again, you can start with your to-do list. But instead of thinking about deadlines and priorities, take a different approach: Think about the sense of accomplishment locked inside each potential Highlight.

Look for activities that are not urgent. Instead, consider projects you've been meaning to get around to but haven't quite found the time. Maybe you have a particular skill you want to put to use, or maybe it's a pet project that you want to develop before sharing it with the world. These projects are super vulnerable to procrastination, because although they're important, they are not time-sensitive, and that makes them easy to postpone. Use your Highlight to break the "someday" cycle.

Here are some examples of Satisfying Highlights:

- Finish the proposal for a new work project you're excited about and share it with a few trusted colleagues.
- Research destinations for your next family vacation.
- Draft 1,500 words of the next chapter in your novel.

Joy

The third strategy focuses on joy: **When I reflect on today, what will bring me the most joy?**

Not every hour has to be optimized and orchestrated for maximum efficiency. One of our goals with Make Time is to steer you away from the impossible vision of perfectly planned days and toward a life that's more joyful and less reactive. That means doing some things just because you like doing them.

To other people, some of your joyful Highlights may look like wastes of time: sitting at home reading a book, meeting a friend to play Frisbee in the park, even doing a crossword puzzle. Not to us. You only waste time if you're not intentional about how you spend it.

All sorts of Highlights can bring you joy. Here are some examples:

- Going to your friends' housewarming party
- Mastering a new song on the guitar
- Having a fun lunch with your hilarious coworker
- Taking your kid to the playground

Trust Your Gut to Choose the Best Highlight

Which strategy should you use on any particular day? We think the best way to choose a Highlight is to trust your gut to decide whether an urgent, joyful, or satisfying Highlight is best for *today*.[2]

A good rule of thumb is to **choose a Highlight that takes sixty to ninety minutes**. If you spend less than sixty minutes, you might not have time to get in the zone, but after ninety minutes of focused attention, most people need a break. Sixty to ninety minutes is a sweet spot. It's enough time to do something meaningful, and it's a reasonable amount of time to create in your schedule. With the tactics in this chapter and throughout the book, we're confident you can make sixty to ninety minutes for your Highlight.

When you're starting out, choosing a Highlight may feel strange or difficult. If this happens to you, don't worry; it's perfectly natural. Over time, you'll get the hang of it and choosing will become easier and easier. Remember, you really can't screw it up. And because Make Time is a daily system, no matter what happens, you can always tweak your approach and try again tomorrow.

Of course, your Highlight isn't magical. Deciding where to focus your energy on any particular day isn't going to make it happen automatically. But being intentional is an essential step toward making more time in your life. Choosing a Highlight makes focusing on your

---

2   Of course, if something falls into *all three* categories, you should probably make that your Highlight!

priorities the default, so you can spend time and energy on what matters, not on reacting to the distractions and demands of modern life.

Jake

It's never too late in the day to choose (or change) your Highlight. Recently, I had a really lousy day. In the morning, I'd planned to make my Highlight editing 100 pages of the *Make Time* manuscript. But all day long I was randomized by everything from a plumbing problem to a pounding headache to unexpected dinner guests. In the afternoon, I realized I could change my Highlight—and my attitude. I decided to scrap my editing goal for the day and instead focus on enjoying the dinner with friends. When I made that choice, my whole day turned around. I could let go and enjoy.

After losing those winter months in 2008, JZ didn't have a flash of inspiration that led him to the idea of a Highlight. But his observation that daily satisfaction comes from a medium-size Highlight rather than tiny tasks or lofty goals planted the seed that grew into the philosophy we use to plan our days.

Now we both select a Highlight every day[3] and have come up with a bunch of tactics that help us turn our intentions into action. Some are everyday things such as scheduling your Highlight (#1), and others

---

3   Well, *almost* every day. Remember, it's okay to fall off the wagon.

are occasional, like stringing together multiple daily Highlights into a sort of personal sprint (#7).

The next section is a collection of tactics for choosing a Highlight and making time for it in your day. As you read the tactics on the following pages, remember the mantra Pick, Test, Repeat. Make a note of the tactics that sound helpful, fun, and a little challenging. If you're just starting with Make Time, focus on one Highlight tactic at a time. If it works, keep it in your routine. If you need additional help choosing and making time for your Highlight, come back and add another tactic you want to try. Now let's start highlighting the people, projects, and work that matter most to you.

Choose Your Highlight

1. Write It Down

2. Groundhog It (or, "Do Yesterday Again")

3. Stack Rank Your Life

4. Batch the Little Stuff

5. The Might-Do List

6. The Burner List

7. Run a Personal Sprint

1. Write It Down

Yes, we know this sounds obvious, but there's a special, almost magical power to writing down your plans: The things you write down are more likely to happen. If you want to make time for your Highlight, start by writing it down.

Make writing down your Highlight a simple daily ritual. You can do it at any time, but the evening (before bed) and the morning work best for most people. JZ likes to think about tomorrow's Highlight as he's winding down in the evening. Jake chooses his Highlight in the morning, sometime between eating breakfast and starting work.

Where should you record your Highlight? You've got plenty of options. There are apps (check our recommendations at maketimebook .com) that will remind you to write it down every day. You can put your Highlight on your calendar as an all-day event. You can jot it down in a notebook. But if we had to pick one method for writing down a Highlight, we'd choose sticky notes. They're easy to get and easy to use, and they don't require batteries or software updates.

You can write down your Highlight and never look at it again—or you can stick it to your laptop, phone, fridge, or desk as a persistent but gentle reminder of the one big thing you want to make time for today.

2. Groundhog It (or, "Do Yesterday Again")

Not sure what to choose for your Highlight? Just like Bill Murray in the movie *Groundhog Day*, you can do yesterday again. There are lots of great reasons to repeat your Highlight:

- If you didn't get to your Highlight, it's probably still important. **Repeat for a second chance.**
- If you started your Highlight but didn't finish it or if your Highlight was part of a bigger project, today is the perfect day to make progress or start a personal sprint (#7). **Repeat to build momentum.**
- If you're establishing a new skill or routine, you'll *need* repetition to cement the behavior. **Repeat to create a habit.**
- If yesterday's Highlight brought you joy or satisfaction, hey, there's nothing wrong with more of that! **Repeat to keep the good times rolling.**

You don't have to reinvent yourself each day. Once you've identified something that's important to you, focusing on it day after day will help it take root in your life, grow, and flourish. Sounds cheesy, but it's true.

3. Stack Rank Your Life

If you're feeling stuck choosing a Highlight or if you're feeling a conflict between competing priorities in your life, try this recipe for ranking your big priorities:

Ingredients
- 1 pen
- 1 piece of paper (or the notes app on your phone)

1. Make a list of the big things that matter in your life.

We don't just mean at work. This list can include "Friends" or "Family" or "Parenting"; it can include your significant other—or, if you're in the market for a significant other, "Dating." You might list hobbies ("Soccer," "Painting") alongside work. Your big things can be as broad as "Work" or as specific as "Get promoted" or "Apollo project." Other categories to consider are health, finances, and personal growth.
- Include only big stuff and try to use one- or two-word titles (this keeps the list high level).
- Don't prioritize the list yet, just write it.
- List three to ten things. Then . . .

2. Choose the one most important thing.

This is easier said than done, but you can do it! Here are some tips:

- Consider what's most meaningful to you, not what is most urgent.
- Think about what needs the most effort or work. For example, exercise might be very important, but if you already have a strong habit in place, you might shift your focus elsewhere.
- Follow your heart. For example, you might think you should put "Work" ahead of "Fiddle lessons" but you really wish you could make the fiddle your top priority. Well, do it!
- Don't sweat it—this list isn't set in stone. You can always make a new stack rank next month, next week, tomorrow, or even later this afternoon.
- Once you've chosen the most important thing . . .

3. Choose the second, third, fourth, and fifth most important things.

4. Rewrite the list in order of priority.

5. Draw a circle around number one.

If you want to make progress on your number one priority, you'll need to make it your focus whenever possible. Drawing the circle reinforces this prioritization—there's something symbolic about putting your decision in ink.

6. Use this list to help you choose Highlights.

Keep this list around to remind yourself of your one highest priority—and to break ties between two activities when you're not sure how to spend your effort.

Jake

I'll share a couple of my own lists. First, from August 2017:

1. Family
2. Write *Make Time*
3. Write novel
4. Advising and workshops

One month later, in September, I reshuffled my list:

1. Write *Make Time*
2. Family
3. Advising and workshops
4. Write novel

Yes, I demoted my family to number 2. What a jerk! But I knew I had to put the pedal to the metal on *Make Time* so that we could finish the manuscript before JZ left town to sail to Mexico in October. And my family was in a good spot—my kids were back in school after a summer in which we did a bunch of projects and traveled together, and we had good defaults in place for spending time together. Shifting family to number two didn't mean ignoring them; it just meant being honest with myself about where I most needed to focus.

4. Batch the Little Stuff

It can be tough to focus on your Highlight when you know there are dozens of non-Highlight tasks piling up. We have the same problem. In fact, JZ's Highlight today is to finish a draft of this tactic, but at some point this week he also has to catch up on email (he got behind while traveling last week) and return a few phone calls.

Fortunately, we have a solution: Bundle up the small tasks and use batch processing to get them all done in one Highlight session. In other words, make a batch of small things your big thing. For example, one day this week, JZ's Highlight will be "catch up on email" or "return phone calls."

These small tasks may not sound like Highlight material—no one wishes they could make time for email—but there's a surprising satisfaction that comes from catching up. And when you catch up all at once instead of constantly trying to keep your inbox or to-do list empty, you supercharge that feeling of satisfaction.

Just don't do it every day. This is a once-in-a-while tactic, a way of dealing with the necessary chores and tasks that otherwise invade our days. You'll realize the real power of this tactic on the days you *don't* use it: knowing you can safely ignore small, nonurgent tasks, letting them pile up while you focus on your Highlight. After all, with batching the little stuff, you have a plan for catching up.

Tactic Battle: To-Do Lists

Remember, not all tactics work for all people, and that goes for the two of us. Sometimes we disagree on whether a tactic really worked (do I have more energy because I took a caffeine nap [#72] or just because I took a nap?). Sometimes we have very different objective results. But rather than water down our opinions, when we disagree, we'll present our conflicting advice head to head so that you can experiment and decide for yourself where you stand.

Here's one thing we do agree on: We hate to-do lists. Checking off finished tasks feels good, but the fleeting glow of accomplishment masks an ugly truth: Most to-dos are just reactions to other people's priorities, not yours. And no matter how many tasks you finish, you're never done—more to-dos are always waiting to take their place. To-do lists just perpetuate the feeling of "unfinishedness" that dogs modern life.

To-do lists also can obscure what's really important. We're all susceptible to choosing the path of least resistance, especially when we're tired, stressed, overwhelmed, or just plain busy. To-do lists make it worse because they mix easy tasks with hard-but-important ones.

When you use a to-do list, you're tempting yourself to put off those important tasks and knock off one of the easy items instead.

But to-do lists aren't all bad. They let you capture things so you don't have to hold them all in your brain. To-do lists let you see everything in one place. They're a necessary evil.

So as much as we dislike to-do lists, we have to use them. Over the years, we've both developed our own special to-do-list technique. Naturally, each of us thinks his solution is the best, so we'll let you decide.

5. The Might-Do List

JZ

My solution to the to-do-list problem is to separate the decision about what to do from the act of doing it. I call my approach the Might-Do List. It's exactly what it sounds like: a list of things you *might do*. Projects sit on your Might-Do List until you decide to make them your Highlight and schedule them on your calendar. Here's how the pieces fit together:

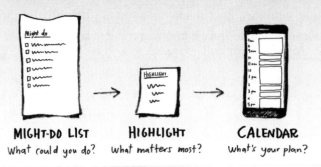

MIGHT-DO LIST	HIGHLIGHT	CALENDAR
What could you do?	What matters most?	What's your plan?

You're especially vulnerable to path-of-least-resistance thinking when you don't plan. But when you take an important task off your Might-Do List, make it your daily Highlight, and put it on your calendar, you'll know you made a thoughtful decision about how to spend your time, and you can pour your energy into the task at hand.

A Might-Do List can help you avoid the to-do-list treadmill at the office or on personal projects. In 2012, my wife and I bought our first sailboat together. In 2016, we sold that boat and bought a different one. Each time, we were taking on not just a boat but a big project. There were literally hundreds of to-dos required to get the boats ready, from the trivial (install towel hooks) to the intense (sterilize the plumbing so it's safe for drinking water). If we had worked directly from our to-do list, we would have been overwhelmed. Instead, we used a Might-Do List to help us stay organized (and sane!) and ensure that we were making time for the important tasks rather than frittering away day after day on the easy stuff.

Here's how it worked: Before a day of boat work, we'd sit down with our Might-Do List and talk about everything we *could* do. We'd use the same three Highlight criteria— urgency, satisfaction, and joy—to select the work that was important to do *today*. Then we'd put it on the calendar, using our best guess at the time required. When the specified time rolled around, we'd show up at our boat, tools and coffee in hand, with a plan for the day. This helped us stay intentional and focused and allowed us to finish each day with a deep sense of satisfaction and accomplishment.

6. The Burner List

Jake

I love the idea of JZ's "Might-Do" framework, but I need something more detailed to help me choose and track the most important Highlights. My method is called the Burner List. It won't track every detail of every project or help you juggle a million tasks. But that's exactly the point. The Burner List is intentionally limited. It forces you to acknowledge that you can't take on every project or task that comes your way. Like time and mental energy, the Burner List is limited, and so it forces you to say no when you need to and stay focused on your number one priority. Here's how to make one:

1. Divide a sheet of paper into two columns.
Get out a single blank sheet of paper and create two columns by drawing a line down the middle. The left-hand column is going to be your front burner, and the right-hand column your back burner.

2. Put your most important project on the front burner.
You are allowed to have one and *only* one project, activity, or objective on the front burner. Not two, not three—just one.

In the top left-hand corner, write the name of your most important project and underline it. Then list the to-dos for that top project. This should include any task you can do in the next few days to move the project forward.

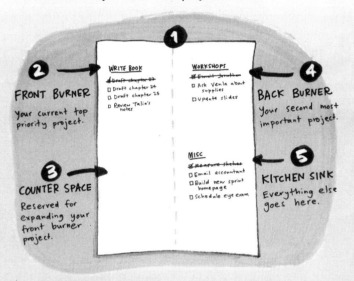

FRONT BURNER
Your current top priority project.

COUNTER SPACE
Reserved for expanding your front burner project.

WRITE BOOK
~~Draft chapter 23~~
☐ Draft chapter 24
☐ Draft chapter 25
☐ Review Talia's notes

WORKSHOPS
~~Email Jonathan~~
☐ Ask Venla about supplies
☐ Update slides

BACK BURNER
Your second most important project.

MISC
~~Measure shelves~~
☐ Email accountant
☐ Build new sprint homepage
☐ Schedule eye exam

KITCHEN SINK
Everything else goes here.

3. Leave some counter space.

Leave the rest of the first column empty. It might be tempting to fill the space with every task you can think of, but the Burner List is not intended to fill the paper's surface area efficiently; it's intended to make good use of your time and energy. The blank space gives you room to add more tasks for the top project as they come up, but just as important, extra visual space makes it easier to focus on the important stuff.

4. Put your second most important project on the back burner.

At the top of the right-hand column, write the name of your second most important project and underline it, then list the related to-dos underneath.

The idea is to direct your time and attention as you would if you were cooking on a stove. You'd naturally focus most of your attention on the front burner. Sure, you're aware of the back burner and might reach back there to stir a pot or flip a pancake every now and again, but the front burner is where the action is.

5. Make a kitchen sink.
Finally, about halfway down the right-hand column, list any miscellaneous tasks that you need to do but that don't fit with project 1 or project 2. It doesn't matter if they're part of project 3 or project 4 or are totally random; they get chucked into the kitchen sink with everything else.

The Burner List won't have room for everything, and that means you'll have to let go of things that aren't as important. But again, that's exactly the point. I've found that one big project, one small project, and a short list of catchall tasks are all I can (or should!) take on at once. If it doesn't fit on the paper, it won't fit in my life.

The Burner List is disposable and gets scrapped every time I cross off a few finished to-dos. I generally "burn" through a list every few days and then re-create it over and over. This act of re-creating the list is important. It allows me to discard some unfinished tasks that no longer matter, and it also allows me to reconsider which projects belong on the front and back burners *right now*. Sometimes it'll be a work project that gets the high-priority spot, and sometimes it'll be a personal project. It's okay and natural for things to shift. What's important is there can only be one front burner project at a time.

Now get cooking!

7. Run a Personal Sprint

Whenever you begin a project, your brain is like a computer starting up, loading relevant information, rules, and processes into your working memory. This "boot up" takes time, and you have to redo it to a certain extent every time you pick up the project.

This is why, in our design sprints, teams work on the same project for five days in a row. Information stays in people's working memory from one day to the next, allowing them to get deeper and deeper into the challenge. As a result, we can accomplish exponentially more than we could if those same hours were spread across weeks and months.

But this kind of a sprint isn't just for teams; you can run a "personal sprint" yourself. Whether you're painting the living room, learning to juggle, or preparing a report for a new client, you'll do better work and make faster progress if you keep at it for consecutive days. Just choose the same Highlight for several days in a row (breaking it up into steps for each day if you need to) and keep your mental computer running.

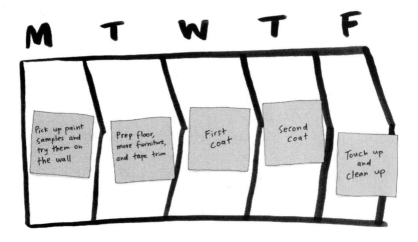

Jake

I've seen this effect with my writing. The first day after a long break is hard. I may not write much of anything, and I get frustrated and cranky. The second day is still slow, but I feel I'm starting to boot up. By the third day and fourth day, I'm in the zone—and I do whatever I can to keep the momentum.

Make Time for Your Highlight

8. Schedule Your Highlight

If you want to make time for your Highlight, start with the calendar. Like writing down your Highlight (#1), this tactic could hardly be simpler:

1. Think about how much time you want for your Highlight.
2. Think about when you want to do your Highlight.
3. Put your Highlight on the calendar.

When you schedule something, you're making a commitment to yourself, sending yourself a tiny message that says: "I'm going to do this." But scheduling your Highlight has another important benefit: It forces you to confront the trade-offs in how you spend your time. Imagine today's Highlight is to buy groceries and cook dinner for your family. You think, "Dinner should be ready at 7 p.m. or the kids won't get to bed in time. And I need to start cooking at 6 p.m. That means I have to leave the office at 5 p.m. so I have time to stop at the store on my way home." You add an event to your calendar at 5 p.m. and label it "Leave work."

Once you've scheduled your Highlight, that time is taken. You can't schedule any meetings or commit to any other activity. When other things come up, you get to decide whether to schedule them in the remaining time around your Highlight or whether they can wait. You can see your priorities take form right there on your calendar.

JZ

Early in my career, I didn't have many meetings, so I never used a calendar. But I had a to-do list. Every day I'd get to the office, take a look at my to-do list, and think, "What should I do today? Ooh, that!" I'd pick out something that seemed easy and time-sensitive and get to work. But by the end of the day, I was often disappointed: I hadn't necessarily done the most important things, and I never finished everything on my to-do list.

Later, I started working at Google. You can't work at Google without using a shared calendar. Not only do you need it to keep track of your meetings (there are a lot), but colleagues also can see your schedule and invite you to meetings by adding them directly to your calendar.

Ironically, it was the busy, meeting-heavy culture of Google—and the required use of a calendar—that helped me make time for things that were important to me. With a calendar, I could see how I was spending my time, and my colleagues could see, too. And as my schedule got crazier, I realized I had to schedule my Highlight if I wanted to make time for it.

9. Block Your Calendar

If you start with an empty calendar, you can schedule your Highlight for the ideal time, when your energy is highest and your focus is at its peak. But for most of us, starting the day with a blank calendar is about as likely as finding a thousand-dollar bill on the sidewalk: It certainly *could* happen, but we'd better not count on it.[4] And if you work in an office where colleagues can add meetings to your calendar, forget about it. You'll have to take a different approach: **Use daily "do not schedule" blocks to make room for your Highlight.**

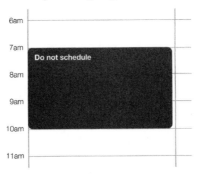

JZ learned this trick from his friend Graham Jenkin. In 2007 and 2008, Graham was JZ's boss at Google, and to JZ, it seemed like Graham could do it all. He managed something like twenty people, and he gave each of them personal attention and true support. He also led the redesign of AdWords, Google's flagship advertising product. This meant he was involved in everything from designing user interfaces, to testing with customers and reviewing specifications, to coordinating with engineers. Everyone wondered where Graham found the time, and most people (including JZ) assumed he worked really long hours. But they were wrong.

---

4   According to the indubitable Wikipedia, "As of May 30, 2009, only 336 $10,000 bills were known to exist; 342 remaining $5,000 bills; and 165,372 remaining $1,000 bills." So keep your eyes open!

In many ways, Graham had the typical schedule of a corporate manager. Each day was packed with meetings. But there was something unusual about his calendar: From 6 to 11 a.m. each day, Graham had scheduled time with *himself*.

"That's my time. I wake up early, get to the office early, hit the gym, grab breakfast, then work for a couple hours before my meetings begin," Graham said.

"Don't people schedule over it?" JZ asked.

"Sometimes they try, but I just tell them I've already got plans."

Ten years later, we still use Graham's trick to make time for our Highlight. And we picked up a few more tips along the way.

Play offense, not defense. Don't use your "do not schedule" blocks just to avoid coworkers or get out of meetings. Be very intentional with any time you block—turn it into Energize time (see page 163) or Highlight time.

Don't be greedy. We *did* say you should block your calendar, but you shouldn't fill it up entirely. It's good to leave unblocked space for opportunities, and your coworkers will appreciate your availability. When you start out with this tactic, you might try blocking an hour or two each day and then adjust from there.

Take it seriously. If you don't take those commitments seriously, other people won't either. Treat these blocks like important meetings, and when people try to double-book you, remember Graham's simple and effective comeback: "I've already got plans."

10. Bulldoze Your Calendar

If you can't block your calendar, there's another way to clear time for your Highlight: Bulldoze it.

Imagine a tiny bulldozer driving through your calendar, pushing events around. The bulldozer might compress one meeting by fifteen minutes and another by thirty. It might shove your one-on-one from the morning to the afternoon or push your lunch back by half an hour so you can get a full two hours of Highlight time. The bulldozer could even stack all your meetings on one or two days of the week, freeing up the other days for solo work.

Bulldozing is admittedly easier if you're the boss than it is if you're the intern,[5] but you might have more control over your calendar than you think. There's no harm in telling people something important came up and asking if they can meet a little earlier or later or for a quick chat instead of for an hour. In fact, when meetings are shortened or disappear from the calendar, people are usually thrilled.

We all try to say yes to meeting requests because that's the default in virtually every office culture. But don't assume there's a good reason behind the length of every meeting or the time of day it shows up on your calendar or even why *you* were invited. Office schedules aren't formed by some grand design; they congeal organically, like pond scum. It's okay to clean things up.

11. Flake It Till You Make It

There will be days and weeks when you feel so busy and overscheduled that you can't imagine how you'll ever make time for your Highlight.

---

5   Although if you can get the CEO to reschedule the quarterly all-hands to make time for your nap, hey, more power to you.

When this happens, ask yourself what you can cancel. Can you skip a meeting, push back a deadline, or ditch your plans with a friend?

We know, we know. This mindset sounds horrible. Even the *New York Times* bemoaned today's culture of last-minute cancellation, calling this the "Golden Age of Bailing."

You know what? We think bailing is fine provided that you do something worthwhile instead. Of course, you can't skip out on everything all the time, but there's a big middle ground between blindly serving your calendar and being an unreliable flake.

Just be honest, explain why you're bailing, and let it go. Bailing is not a good long-term strategy; over time, you'll get a feel for how many commitments you can take on while still making time for your Highlight. But in the meantime, it's better to ruffle a few feathers than to always push your priorities off for "someday." Go ahead and flake out. Don't feel bad. And if people complain, just tell them we said it was okay.

12. Just Say No

Blocking, bulldozing, and flaking are great ways to make time for your Highlight. But the best way to get out of low-priority obligations is never to accept them in the first place.

For the two of us, saying no doesn't come naturally. We're the kind of people who default to yes. This is partly niceness—we wish we could do it all, and we want to be helpful. And to be honest, it's partly a lack of guts. It's much *easier* to say yes. Saying no to an invitation or a new project can feel uncomfortable, and we've lost many hours, days, and weeks of Highlight time because we didn't have the courage to decline a commitment up front.

But we've been working on it, and we've found that we're much happier when we default to no. What helped us make the switch was developing scripts for various situations so that we always know *how* to say no.

Are you already fully committed to your Highlight and truly don't have time? "Sorry, I'm really busy with some big projects, and I just don't have time for anything new."

Could you squeeze in a new project but worry about giving it the proper attention? "Unfortunately, I don't have the time to do a great job on this."

Invited to an activity or event that you know you won't enjoy? "Thanks for the invitation, but I'm not really into softball."[6]

In short, **be nice but honest.** Over the years, we've heard about many tricky techniques for deflecting requests, making up excuses, or deferring indefinitely, and we've tried some of them. But they don't feel good, and they're not honest. Worse, they just delay the hard decision until a later time, and those half choices can weigh you down, sticking to you like barnacles on the hull of a boat. So ditch the tricks, shed the barnacles, and tell the truth.

Just because you're saying no to this request doesn't mean you can't say yes in the future. Again, say it only if you mean it. "I really appreciate the invitation, and I'd love to hang out another time." Or "It means a lot that you'd ask for my help, and I hope we can work together in the future."

Our friend Kristen Brillantes uses what she calls the Sour Patch Kid method when she says no. Just like the candy, Kristen's answers are sour at first but sweet at the end. For example: "Unfortunately, my team won't be able to participate. But you might ask Team X; they'd be perfect for this kind of event." The key, says Kristen, is to make

---

6   When you're saying no to a friend, you can try humorous bluntness. Friend: "Want to run timed miles at the track before work tomorrow?" You: "HELL NO."

sure the sweet ending is authentic, not an empty add-on. If she can, she'll offer a connection to another person with capacity or interest for whom the invitation might be a cool opportunity. If not, she offers encouragement or gratitude. Something as simple as a "Thank you for thinking of me; this sounds really fun" goes a long way.

13. Design Your Day

When we ran our design sprints for Google Ventures, we planned each day hour by hour and even minute by minute. Every sprint was another opportunity to perfect our formula. We kept track of the ebbs and flows of work throughout the day—when people's energy dipped, when things moved too fast or too slow—and adjusted accordingly.

Blocking your calendar and scheduling your Highlight is a great way to start making time. But you can take this proactive, intentional mindset to another level by learning from our sprints and designing your *entire* day. JZ has been doing this for years, structuring the time in his calendar like this:

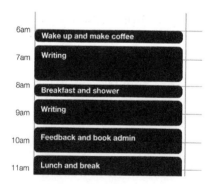

Yes, it's detailed. Very detailed. He actually blocked time for making coffee and showering! JZ designs his time like this nearly every day. In the evening, he looks back and quickly evaluates his schedule for what worked and what didn't and compares his plan with how he really spent his time. Then he adjusts his future schedule to account for what he's learned.

Being this scheduled might sound annoying: "Where's the freedom and spontaneity, man?" But in reality, a structured day creates freedom. When you don't have a plan, you have to decide constantly what to do next, and you might get distracted thinking about all the things you should or could do. But a completely planned day provides the freedom to focus on the moment. Instead of thinking about *what* to do next, you're free to focus on *how* to do it. You can be in the flow, trusting the plan set out by your past self. When is the best time of day to check email? How long should it take? You can design the answers ahead of time rather than reacting in real time.

Jake

Sarah Cooper is one of my role models. A few years ago, she quit her job at Google to become a full-time writer and comedian and then promptly started cranking out hilarious posts on her website *The Cooper Review*, racked up millions of readers, and signed a deal for three books. So naturally, when I quit *my* job at Google, I went to Sarah for advice on how she scheduled her time now that she wasn't working in an office.

Sarah's secret was establishing a solid, predictable schedule by designing her day hour by hour. She used a notebook for planning her schedule and evaluating what really did or didn't get done afterward. "It made me realize there are actually enough hours in the day to get stuff done. Instead of writing to-do lists, I map out my day in half-hour increments."

I liked the idea and I knew all about JZ's freakish devotion to micromanaging his calendar, so I gave it a shot. Rather than using my calendar or a journal, I used an approach recommended by Cal Newport in *Deep Work:* writing my schedule on a piece of blank paper, then replanning throughout the day as things change and evolve, like this:

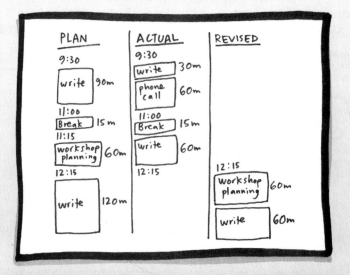

It worked. The constant redesigning gave me a handle on how I was spending my time, showed me when my best writing time was, and helped me establish a routine. Now, when I feel things are out of whack, I know what to do—it's time to redesign my day.

Tactic Battle: Morning vs. Night

If you can't make time for your Highlight in the middle of the day, you might try creating some space in the early morning or late evening. JZ's a night owl who turned himself into a morning person. Jake couldn't make the switch, so he optimized the night. Here are our strategies.

14. Become a Morning Person

JZ

In 2012, I decided to become a morning person.

It didn't come naturally. My whole life, whenever I had to wake early—for a meeting, event, or class—I struggled to get out of bed. I always seemed to be rushing and running late, and the feeling of foggy, zombielike fatigue loomed over my day like a hangover.

But I was fascinated by the potential of mornings. Those early hours seemed like a gift: a couple of "free" hours when I could work on my Highlight and prepare for the day. Becoming a morning person also would give me more time with my wife, who worked at a company in which early meetings were the norm. I hated keeping a different schedule from Michelle, and it cut into our time together.

As a natural night owl, I knew I needed a plan if I wanted to avoid the groggy, unfocused feeling of my previous early mornings. So I decided to research what had worked for other people and try some simple experiments.

It worked. With the help of a couple of easy tricks, I traded a typical night-owl schedule—up till midnight or later, staring at a screen, doing design work, writing, coding—for an uncommon routine in which I go to sleep early, wake up early, and often use the quiet morning hours for my daily Highlight.

Here are the tricks I'd share with any night owls who want to start waking early.

Start with Light, Coffee, and Something to Do

Don't underestimate the importance of light in waking up. Humans are hardwired to wake when it's light and get sleepy when it's dark. But if you want to make time for your Highlight before the workday, you can't wait for sunrise; for most of the year in much of the world, you need to wake before dawn. So when I wake up, I turn on every light in my apartment (or boat when I'm living aboard). And I try to always watch the sunrise, even if it's an hour or two after I get up; seeing the sky go from dark to light reminds my brain that it's time to transition from night to day.

Coffee is also super important to me. Sure, the caffeine is nice, but the preparation routine is essential to my morning. It takes me fifteen minutes to make coffee using a simple pour-over technique: boil water, grind beans, position filter, add grounds, pour water. This process is more labor-intensive than using a machine, but that's the idea. My slow coffee ritual keeps me occupied during the low-willpower period when I would otherwise check email or look at Twitter, both of which are likely to send me into a reactive vortex of unproductivity. Instead, I stand in the kitchen (or galley), wake up slowly, think about my day, and enjoy a fresh cup of coffee while I settle in to work on my Highlight.

Giving yourself something to do in the morning will help you wake up early, but for me it's also *why* I wake up early. Even on the days when I don't work on my daily Highlight first thing in the morning, I still find reasons to make time in those predawn hours. Exercise is a great morning activity. Even doing dishes, ironing shirts, or straightening up around the house helps me wake up and feel productive before the day has started.

However, even with light, coffee, and something to do, it's tough to wake up early without making some adjustments to your evening routine.

Design the Nights Before

Start with an honest assessment of how much sleep you need and how much you get. I feel best after seven to eight hours of sleep (and sometimes nine, especially in the winter). Most days I wake up around 5:30 a.m., so that means I need to go to bed around 9:30 p.m. If you're a night owl, you might think it's impossible to fall asleep this early. So did I. But for most of us, it's society, not our bodies, that dictates our default bedtime. If you want to try resetting that default, here are a few tips that can help.

Pay attention to how food and drink affect your sleep. There's plenty of evidence that alcohol does not improve sleep quality even though it might feel that way, and it particularly impairs REM sleep. I enjoy dark chocolate after dinner (see #69), but I learned the hard way about its surprising caffeine content.

Finally, adjust your environment to wind down and signal "bedtime" to your body. I begin by lowering the lights. I turn off peripheral lights in the kitchen and foyer, then switch to floor lamps in the living room and bedroom. My favorite routine—and dorkiest by far—is a do-it-yourself turn-down service. Around 7 p.m. each night, I close the curtains in the bedroom, remove the decorative pillows from the bed, and pull back the covers. (Check out #84, "Fake the Sunset," for more.)

It's not always easy for me to wake up at 5:30 a.m., but I've learned to love mornings. And the payoff is amazing; by 9:30 a.m. most days I've had an hour of productive work, showered and dressed, walked two miles, had breakfast, and enjoyed two cups of coffee.

Becoming a morning person is not for everyone. Some people will have more success making time at night. Still, it's worth giving it a shot. After all, I didn't know I *could be* a morning person until I tried. Sometimes we don't know what we're capable of until we apply some simple tactics and an experimental mindset to our lives.

15. Nighttime Is Highlight Time

Jake

We're genetically predisposed to be either morning people or night people. I base this not on science but on firsthand observation of my sons conducted over the past several thousand days.

My older son, Luke, is a morning person who wakes up singing. At breakfast, he can speak at a rate of approximately 2,600 words per minute, and that's without any coffee. My son Flynn, in contrast, is a night person. The morning makes him confused and angry, and if I try to talk to him before 7 a.m., he will punch me in the crotch.

I get it. I'm a night person, too. I tried JZ's tactics to become a morning person but was always thwarted by interruptions from my kids. It was frustrating. With a family and a full-time job, it was often tough to find uninterrupted time during the day to do my Highlight. If the mornings were unavailable, I'd have to make the time somewhere else.

I decided to get better at being a night person. I realized that the hours between 9:30 p.m. (when my kids were asleep) and 11:30 p.m. (when I went to sleep) could be the perfect time to focus. I'd never taken nighttime seriously before, but there were two bonus hours just sitting there for the taking if only I could use them effectively.

The biggest challenge was that even though I could

easily stay awake till 11:30 p.m., my battery was often drained. I didn't have the mental focus to do anything significant, so I was in the habit of squandering those bonus hours on low-energy, low-benefit activities such as checking email and reading about the Seattle Seahawks.

It took me a while to figure out how to handle this challenge, but in the end I came up with a three-part strategy for turning nighttime into Highlight time:

Recharge First
If I'm planning to stay up and work on a project, I'll start by refreshing my brain with a real break (#80). After my younger son goes to bed (around 8:30 p.m.), I might sit down with my wife and older son and watch part of a movie. Or I might read a few pages in a novel. Or I might clean the kitchen and put away toys in the living room. These activities take my mind out of "busy mode" and recharge my mental battery—a major difference from the frenzy of checking email, reading clickbait news articles, or watching an intense TV show designed to suck me into a black hole of binge watching.[7]

Go Offline
Around nine-thirty, I'll switch into Highlight mode, usually for writing but sometimes to prepare a presentation or workshop. Even with a quick battery recharge, my focus is usually not at 100 percent, so I put a vacation timer on the Internet (#28), allowing me to concentrate on my writing with minimal willpower.

---

7   For an insightful look at the science of binge watching and cliffhangers, check out Adam Alter's book *Irresistible*.

Don't Forget to Wind Down

I learned the hard way that I have to spin down my brain after late-night work or I'll seriously mess up my sleep. Dimming the lights (#84) helps, but most important is getting to bed before I turn into a pumpkin. For me, that magic hour is 11:30 p.m., and if I'm not in bed by then, I'll tank my energy the next day.

16. Quit When You're Done

It can be hard to stop work at the end of the day, because the Busy Bandwagon encourages a "just one more thing" mentality. One more email. One more to-do. Many people quit only when they're too exhausted to go on, and even so, they check email again before they go to bed.

Hey, we fall into that trap ourselves. The Busy Bandwagon does a great job of convincing us all that "just one more thing" is the responsible and hardworking thing to do, and often it seems like the only way to keep from falling behind.

But it isn't. Working till exhaustion makes us *more* likely to fall behind by robbing us of the rest we need to prioritize and do our best work. Trying to cram in just one more thing is like driving a car that is running out of gas: No matter how long you keep your foot on the accelerator, if the tank is empty, you aren't going anywhere. You need to stop and refuel.

In our design sprints, we found that if we ended each workday *before* people were exhausted, the week's productivity increased dramatically. Even shortening the day by thirty minutes made a big difference.

When should you quit? Instead of trying to answer every email (not happening) or finish every task (dream on), you need to create your own finish line. Perhaps you can find a perfect time of day to stop—in our design sprints, we used 5 p.m. as our cutoff.

Or you can use your Highlight. As quitting time approaches, think about whether you accomplished your Highlight. If you have, you can rest knowing you made time for the day's most important job. No matter how much you did or didn't get done or how many hours you did or didn't work, you'll be able to look back on the day with a sense of joy, accomplishment, or satisfaction—or all three!

And if you *didn't* finish your Highlight, you (hopefully) had to bump it for some unforeseen super important project. If that's the case, you can still feel satisfied knowing you did something urgent and necessary. Good job! Now let yourself ignore that inbox and call it a day.

JZ

Back in 2005, I started working at a tech startup in Chicago. It was my first full-time office job and the first time I had to figure out how to manage my energy throughout a long workday. I quickly learned that it was easier for me to focus on work in the hours before lunch, so when I found myself struggling with a not-so-hard task late in the day, I'd give myself permission to quit and pick it up again in the morning. Almost every time, I'd breeze through and finish in a fraction of the time it would've taken me the previous night. Instead of trying to power through when I was running on fumes, I refueled by quitting when I was done.

Laser

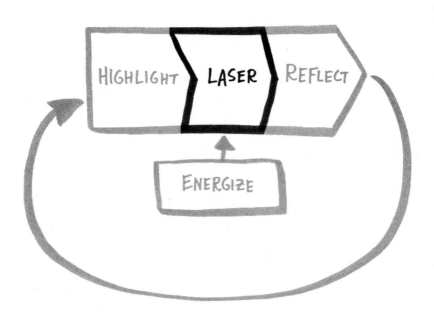

> To pay attention,
> this is our endless and proper work.
>
> —MARY OLIVER

Okay, you've chosen a Highlight for the day and you've made time for it in your busy schedule. Now that time has arrived, and you need to focus. And, of course, *this* is the hard part.

This chapter is about a state of mind called Laser. When you're in Laser mode, your attention is focused on the present like a laser beam shining on a target. You're in the flow, fully engaged and immersed in the moment. When you're laser-focused on your Highlight, it feels fantastic—it's the payoff for proactively choosing what's important to you.

The word *Laser* might sound intense, but if you've chosen a Highlight and cleared time, there doesn't have to be anything hard or complicated about it. When you're doing something you care about and have the energy to focus, Laser mode simply appears.

Unless . . . you get distracted. Distraction is the enemy of Laser mode. It's like a giant disco ball in the path of your laser beam: Light goes everywhere *except* in the direction of the target. When that happens, you can easily end up missing out on your Highlight.

We don't know about you, but the two of us get distracted. A lot. We get distracted by email. We get distracted by Twitter. We get distracted by Facebook. We get distracted by sports news, political news, tech news, and searching for the perfect animated GIF. We even got distracted while writing *this* chapter.[1]

We hope you won't judge us too harshly; after all, it's a distracting world out there. There's always something new in our inbox, on the Web, or on that shiny smartphone in our pocket, and we just can't resist: Apple reports that people unlock their iPhones an average of 80 times per day, and a 2016 study by customer-research firm Dscout found that people touched their phones an average of 2,617 times per day. Distracted has become the new default.

In this world, willpower alone is not enough to protect your focus. We're not saying this because we don't have confidence in you or to justify our own weaknesses. We're saying this because we know exactly what you're up against. Remember, we helped *build* two of the stickiest Infinity Pools out there. We've seen the industry of distraction from the inside, and we have a pretty good idea about why this stuff is so irresistible, and how you can redesign the way you use technology to regain control. Here are our stories.

---

1   We eventually got back to it.

A Love Affair with Email

Jake

From the very first moment I saw it—as a high school freshman in 1992—I thought email was just about the coolest thing on earth. Type a message, hit "Send," and the words traveled at the speed of light, immediately appearing on another computer—no matter if it was down the street or halfway around the world. Amazing!

Back when it was still a pretty niche thing that few people knew about, I attempted to impress girls by introducing them to email. "Hey, ladies," I would say, "here's this cool futuristic way to communicate. Send me an email and I'll send you one back!" Surprisingly, this strategy was not successful, and for a long time there wasn't much I could do with email (or girls) except marvel at the possibilities.

Of course, email eventually caught on. By 2000, when I got my first full-time office job, it was the primary form of communication. Even though I was using it mostly for boring work stuff, I still thought there was something magical about sending electronic mail whizzing across the globe.

When I joined Google in 2007 and got the chance to join the Gmail team, I could hardly believe my good fortune. I couldn't have been much more excited if I'd gotten a job as an astronaut.

Diligently, I designed ways to make Gmail better and easier to use. I worked on functional things, like a system for automatically organizing mail, but also fun things, like a tool for adding emojis to messages and visual themes so that users could personalize their inboxes.

We wanted Gmail to be the best email service out there. And the surest way to measure our progress was to look at how many people used Gmail and how often they did so. When people opened up a new Gmail account to try it out, did they stick around, or did they give up on us? Were they coming back frequently enough that we could be sure they liked it? Were the cool features we were building even useful to people? With giant piles of aggregated data, it was possible to find these things out.

Over time, we could see if Gmail was growing, and we could see whether our experiments were making the product "sticky" enough to keep people interested. I loved this work. Every day was exciting. Every improvement might make the lives of millions of people just a *tiny* bit easier. As corny as it sounds, I believed I was helping to make the world a better place.

 Redesigning YouTube

JZ

In 2009, YouTube was best known to me as a destination for funny cat videos and clips of dogs skateboarding. And I'll be honest: When I was first approached about joining the team as a designer, I wasn't too interested. I knew YouTube was popular, but I didn't see how it could ever be more than just a quirky website.

But as I learned more, I got more excited. Executives explained their vision to create a new kind of television with thousands or millions of channels on every possible topic. Instead of settling for what was being broadcast at the moment, YouTube would offer you channels that perfectly matched your interests. Plus, because anyone could post to it, it would provide a platform for aspiring filmmakers, musicians, and other artists to get exposure for their projects. On YouTube, anyone could be "discovered."

It seemed like a big opportunity, so I decided to sign up. In January 2010, my wife and I moved to San Francisco and I joined the YouTube team.

After starting, I learned how YouTube's new vision translated into the way we measured our work. In the era of skateboarding dogs, it was all about the eyeballs. How many videos were people watching? How often did they click on a related video in the sidebar? But with our focus on channels, we began to care more about the minutes: How much *time* were people spending on YouTube? Were they sticking around for the next video in the channel? It was an entirely new mindset.

In my new job, I also learned how important this work was to the company. My perception of YouTube as a quirky video website was at odds with our huge office, hundreds of talented employees, and intense executive focus. It really hit me when my new team—assembled to redesign YouTube and make it more "channel"-oriented—was granted the use of our CEO's office as a "war room." The CEO! He cared so much about making YouTube better that he was willing to give up his office if it would help our chances.

Our efforts paid off. We launched our big redesign in late 2011, and people started subscribing to channels and spending more time watching videos. By early 2012, the press was reporting on the results. For example, London's *Daily Mail* wrote, "YouTube is successfully transforming into a full-blown web TV service," and cited data showing that viewers were staying 60 percent longer than they had the year before. The *Daily Mail*'s analysis really made our hearts sing: "The shift is credited to YouTube's recent relaunch, which added a focus on TV-like 'Channels' and longer shows."

We were elated. Our redesign of YouTube was a rare project in which vision, strategy, and execution came together exactly as we'd hoped. And just like Jake, my colleagues and I loved our work. Minute by minute, we were bringing a little delight into people's days.

Why Infinity Pools Are So Hard to Resist

Okay, those are our stories. What did you notice? Of course, there's the stereotypical Silicon Valley narrative: a bunch of idealistic nerds striving to build cool technology and change the world. But if you dig deeper into these stories, you'll find secret ingredients that explain the irresistible allure of Infinity Pools.

First, there's passion for technology. That wasn't fake—we felt it then, and we feel it today. Multiply that passion by tens of thousands of tech workers, and you get an idea of how the industry constantly churns out faster, more sophisticated gadgets and technologies. The people making this stuff love their work, and they can't wait to bring the next futuristic thing to life. They truly believe that their technology is improving the world. Naturally, when people are passionate about what they're doing, they do great work. So the first secret ingredient that makes Infinity Pool products such as email and online video so irresistible? They're made with love.

Next, there's the sophisticated measurement and capacity for continuous improvement. At Google, we didn't have to trust our hunches about what people wanted; we could run experiments and get quantitative answers. Were people spending more time watching *these* kinds of videos or *those* kinds of videos? Were they coming back to Gmail day after day after day? If the numbers were up, the improvements were working and our customers were happy. If not, we could try something else. Redesigning and relaunching software isn't exactly easy, but it's a heck of a lot faster than, say, manufacturing a new model of car. So **the second secret ingredient is evolution:** Tech products improve dramatically from one year to the next.

The two of us eventually moved on, but we watched closely from the sidelines. Over time, the competition increased. At first, Gmail was up against Web-based email services such as Hotmail and Yahoo. Eventually, as more people started sending messages through social networks, Gmail competed for attention with Facebook. And as iPhones and Android phones spread, Gmail had to compete with smartphone apps as well.

For YouTube, the competition was even more fierce. YouTube doesn't just compete with other video websites; it competes for your time against music, movies, video games, Twitter, Facebook, and Instagram. And, of course, it competes with television; the average American still watches 4.3 hours of good old-fashioned TV every day.[2] Far

---

2 Note to the rest of the world before you make fun of us Americans: According to a 2015 report by the British telecommunications regulator Ofcom, Brits watch 3.6 hours of TV per day, Koreans 3.2, Swedes 2.5, and Brazilians 3.7. Across fifteen countries, the average was 3 hours and 41 minutes per day. So the USA is number one . . . but you're not far behind.

from fading away, television shows keep getting better, the result of a constant race to crank out the best, most binge-worthy series.

Gmail and YouTube didn't "win" those competitions, but the challenge pushed them to evolve and grow. In 2016, Gmail had 1 billion users. In 2017, YouTube announced that it had reached 1.5 billion users and that on average those users spent over one hour per day watching videos.[3]

Meanwhile, the competition for people's eyeballs keeps getting tougher. In 2016, Facebook announced that its 1.65 billion users spent an average of fifty minutes per day across its services. The same year, Snapchat, a relative newcomer, said its 100 million users spent an average of twenty-five to thirty minutes in the app. And that's to say nothing of other apps and websites. Altogether, in 2017, studies showed Americans used their smartphones more than four hours per day.[4]

This **competition is the third secret ingredient** that makes modern technology so compelling. Each time one service rolls out an irresistible new feature or improvement, it ups the ante for its competitors. If one app or site or game doesn't keep you riveted, you've got an infinite number of options two taps away. Everything is up against everything else all the time. It's survival of the fittest, and the survivors are damn good.

The fourth reason Infinity Pools are so addicting? All these technologies take advantage of the natural wiring of our brains, which evolved

---

3   Fun fact: This means that every day, humans watch over 1.5 billion hours of YouTube. If you played those videos back to back, it would take more than 173,000 years, which is roughly how long *Homo sapiens* has existed. Or, to put it another way, that's a heck of a lot of "Gangnam Style."

4   Actually, a 2017 study by a firm called Flurry found that people were spending over *five* hours per day on their phones. Because studies vary, we went with a more conservative number from Hacker Noon, which analyzed research from Nielsen, comScore, and the Pew Research Center, among others, to arrive at "more than four hours."

in a world without microchips. We evolved to be distractible because it kept us safe from danger (check the flash in your peripheral vision—it might be a stalking tiger or a falling tree!). We evolved to love mysteries and stories because they helped us learn and communicate. We evolved to love gossip and seek social status because that allowed us to form tight-knit protective tribes. And we evolved to love unpredictable rewards, whether from a blackberry bush or a smartphone notification, because the possibility of those rewards kept us hunting and gathering even when we returned home empty-handed. **Our caveman brains are the fourth secret ingredient.** Of course we love email, video games, Facebook, Twitter, Instagram, and Snapchat—it's literally in our DNA.

Don't Wait for Technology to Give Back Your Time

Look, we love technology. But there is a very serious problem here. Combine the four-plus hours the average person spends on their smartphone with the four-plus hours the average person spends watching television, and distraction is a full-time job. Here's where we have to point out the (obvious) fifth secret ingredient: **Tech companies make money when you use their products.** They won't offer you small doses voluntarily; they'll offer you a fire hose. And if these Infinity Pools are hard to resist today, they'll be harder to resist tomorrow.

Just to be clear, there's no evil empire behind it all. We don't believe this is an "us vs. them" situation in which coldly calculating tech companies plot to manipulate their hapless customers while laughing maniacally. We think that's a bit reductionist, and it certainly doesn't match our experience. We've been inside those companies, and they're inhabited by well-meaning nerds who want to make your days better. For the most part, the nerds are doing just that, because the best of modern technology *is* remarkable, *and* delightful, and it *does* make our lives more convenient and more fun. When we use our smartphones to navigate an unfamiliar city, or have a video call with a friend, or download an entire book in mere seconds, it's like having superpowers.[5]

But by default, we don't just get the best of modern technology. We get *all* of it, all the time. We get futuristic superpowers *and* addictive distraction, together, on every screen. The better the technology gets, the cooler our superpowers will become—and the more of our time and attention the machines will steal.

We still believe in the nerds, and we hope they'll find creative ways to deliver more superpowers with less interruption. But no matter what Apple does to the iPhone or Google does to Android, there will always be fierce competition for your attention. You can't wait for companies or government regulators to give your focus back. If you want control, you have to redesign your own relationship with technology.

Create Barriers to Distraction

Product designers like us have spent decades removing barriers to make these products as easy to access as possible. The key to getting into Laser mode and focusing on your Highlight is to *bring those barriers back*.

In the following pages, we'll offer you a variety of tactics designed to make it easier to get into and stay in Laser mode, from setting up your own distraction-free smartphone to rearranging your living room furniture to make TV less convenient.

These tactics are all based on the same philosophy: The best way to defeat distraction is to make it harder to react. By adding a few steps that get in the way of checking Facebook, catching up on the news, or turning on the TV, you can short-circuit the cycle that makes these products so sticky. After just a few days, you'll have a new set of defaults: You'll go from distracted to focused, from reactive to inten-

---

5 For a different, more critical look at the dark side of technology, we again recommend Adam Alter's *Irresistible* and Tristan Harris's humanetech.com website—check out our further reading on page 260.

tional, and from overwhelmed to in control. It's all about creating a little inconvenience. When distraction is hard to access, you don't have to worry about willpower. You can channel your energy into making time instead of wasting it.

When you immerse yourself in Laser mode rather than ping-ponging between distraction and attention, you not only make time for what matters most, you make *higher-quality* time. Every distraction imposes a cost on the depth of your focus. When your brain changes contexts—say, going from painting a picture to answering a text and then back to painting again—there's a switching cost. Your brain has to load a different set of rules and information into working memory. This "boot up" costs at least a few minutes, and for complex tasks, it can take even longer. The two of us have found it can take a couple of hours of uninterrupted writing before we're doing our best work; sometimes it even requires several consecutive *days* before we're in the zone.

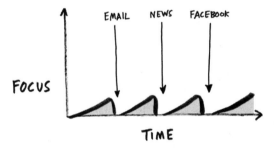

It's like compound interest. The longer you remain focused on your Highlight, the more engaging you'll find it and the better work (or play) you'll do.

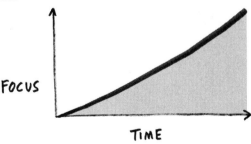

But the benefits of Laser mode aren't just about you and your Highlight. Part of the reason we're all so hooked on distractions is that *everybody else* is, too. It's the fear of missing out—FOMO—and we've all got it. How will we make small talk if we haven't seen the latest HBO series, or read the latest Trump tweets, or studied the cool features of the brand-new iPhone? Everybody else is doing it, and we don't want to get left behind.

We want to encourage you to look at this a bit differently: as an opportunity to stand out, but in a good way. If you change your priorities, people will notice. Your actions show others what's important to you. When your friends, your coworkers, and your kids and family see you being intentional with your time, you'll give *them* permission to question their own "always on" default and step away from their own Infinity Pools. You aren't just making time for yourself and your own Highlight; you're also setting a good example for the people around you.

Next up are our Laser tactics: methods for taking control of your phone, apps, inboxes, and TV, as well as tricks for getting into Laser mode and staying there so you can enjoy your Highlight.

Be the Boss of Your Phone

17. Try a Distraction-Free Phone

> And yet it would be a relief in a way
> not to be bothered with it any more . . .
> Sometimes I have felt it was like an eye looking at me . . .
> I found I couldn't rest without it in my pocket.
>
> —BILBO BAGGINS

Removing email and other Infinity Pool apps from our phones might be the simplest, most powerful change we've made to reclaim time and attention. We've both had distraction-free phones since 2012, and not only have we survived, we've thrived—becoming more effective in our work and just generally enjoying our days more.

Jake

My phone used to call to me from my pocket the way the Ring called to Bilbo Baggins. The second I felt even the slightest twinge of boredom, my phone would appear in the palm of my hand as if by magic. Now, without Infinity Pool apps, I feel less twitchy. Those moments when I used to instinctively reach for my phone, I'm forced to pause— and it turns out those moments are not so boring after all.

But when people learn about our deviant lifestyle, they often think we're nuts. Why don't we just save money and use a flip phone?

Well, here's the thing: Even after you get rid of all the Infinity Pools, a smartphone is *still* a magical device. From maps and driving directions, to music and podcasts, to the calendar and camera, there are plenty of apps that enhance our day-to-day existence without stealing our time.

And we'll be honest: We think smartphones are cool. In addition to being dorks about time, we're also dorks who love gadgets. In 2007,

JZ waited in line for the first iPhone. Ten years later, Jake stayed up into the wee hours to order the iPhone X on its release date. We love our phones—we just don't want everything they offer, all the time. With a distraction-free phone we can turn back the clock to a (slightly) simpler time when it was easier to unplug and sustain attention while *also* enjoying the best of modern technology.

Of course, a distraction-free phone isn't for everyone. To some, the idea of a smartphone without social media, Web browsers, and email sounds nuts, and we're willing to admit that some people might have better self-control than we do. Maybe you don't constantly feel an overpowering urge to pull your phone out of your pocket. Maybe you're firmly in control of your email and newsfeeds rather than the other way around.

All the same, we believe everybody's paying *some* cognitive cost for the constantly updating information at our fingertips. Maybe you don't have a blatant distraction problem the way we do, but there's a good chance your phone's defaults could be more conducive to focus. So even if you already feel in control of your phone, we encourage you to try going distraction-free as a short experiment. It might not stick, but it will give you a chance to reconsider your defaults.

Here, in a nutshell, is how to set up your own distraction-free phone (you can also find a detailed guide with screenshots for both iPhones and Androids on maketimebook.com):

1. Delete social apps.

First, delete Facebook, Instagram, Twitter, Snapchat, and so on (including whatever else has been invented since we wrote this). Don't worry. If you change your mind later, it is *very* easy to install these apps again.

2. Delete other Infinity Pools.

Anything with an infinite supply of interesting content should be deleted. This includes games, news apps, and streaming video like YouTube. If you might refresh it obsessively and/or lose hours without meaning to, get rid of it.

3. Delete email and remove your account.

Email is both an alluring Infinity Pool *and* the beating heart of the Busy Bandwagon. And because it can be difficult to write proper replies to email on the phone (because of time limitations and the challenges of typing on a touch screen), it's often anxiety-provoking as well. We check email on our phones to catch up, but the result is usually just a reminder that we're falling behind. Remove email from your phone and you'll remove a lot of stress along with it.

Email accounts usually are deeply integrated into the device, so in addition to deleting any email apps, you may want to go into your phone's settings and actually remove your email account. Your phone will issue a dire warning about this ("Are you *sure* you want to remove your email account?"), but don't be deterred. Again, if you change your mind later, it's simply a matter of reentering your log-in info.

4. Remove the Web browser.

Finally, you need to disable the Swiss Army knife of distraction: the Web browser. You'll probably have to venture back into the settings to make this change.

5. Keep everything else.

As we mentioned above, there are still lots of amazing apps that are *not* Infinity Pools: ones that make our lives unquestionably more convenient without sucking us into a vortex of distraction. Maps, for example, have an infinite amount of content, but few people are ever tempted to browse maps of random cities. Even apps such as Spotify and Apple Music are relatively harmless; sure, there are an infinite number of songs and podcasts out there, but you're unlikely to be overwhelmed by the urge to surf through the Beatles' back catalog. The same goes for Lyft, Uber, food delivery apps, calendar apps, weather apps, productivity apps, and travel apps. Bottom line: If an app is a tool or if it doesn't make you twitchy, keep it.

Again, your distraction-free phone can be an experiment; you don't need to commit to it for the rest of your life. Give it twenty-four hours, a week, or even a month. Of course, there will be times when you sincerely *have to* use your email or a browser, and when that happens, you can temporarily reenable the apps you need for the task at hand. The key thing here is that you're using your phone intentionally—it's not using you. And when you're done, you set the default back to "off."

We think you'll love life with a distraction-free phone. As one reader who was just getting started said, "I spent the past week with a disabled iPhone, and it's been WONDERFUL. I thought I would miss it so much more than I do." Another reader used a time-tracking app to record her iPhone usage before and after going distraction-free and was shocked by the result: "Getting rid of email and Safari is consistently getting me off my phone for an extra 2.5 hours each day, and on some days way more." That's pretty amazing; imagine recovering one or two hours per day with such a simple change!

The most important reward of a distraction-free phone is reclaiming control. Once you control the defaults, you're the boss. And that's how it should be.

18. Log Out

Typing in your username and password is a hassle, so websites and apps make sure you don't have to do it very often. They encourage you to stay logged in, leaving the door to distraction wide open.

But you can change the default. When you're done using email, Twitter, Facebook, or whatever, log out. The option is available on every website and also in every app on every smartphone. It might not be obvious, but it's always possible. And next time they ask if you want to "Remember me on this device," don't check the box.

JZ

Logging out wasn't enough of a speed bump for my distractible brain, so I supercharged this tactic by changing my passwords to something crazy, annoying to type, and impossible to remember. Personally, I like e$yQK@iYu, but that's just me. I store my passwords in a password manager app so that I can sign in if necessary, but it's intentionally a hassle. Remember, adding friction is the key to avoiding Infinity Pools and staying in Laser mode.

19. Nix Notifications

I do not like this one so well. All he does is yell, yell, yell. . . .
This one is quiet as a mouse. I like to have him in the house.
—DR. SEUSS

App makers are very pushy when it comes to notifications. Who can blame them? All the other apps are doing it. And with everything else screaming for your attention, if they aren't pushy, how would you possibly remember their app exists? You'd probably use it only when you *needed* to. What a darned shame![6]

Notifications are not your friends. They're nonstop attention thieves. Whether or not you try a distraction-free phone, you should at the very least **turn off almost all notifications.** Here's how.

1. Go into your phone's settings, find the list of notifications, and turn them off one by one.
2. Leave only the really critical and useful ones enabled, such as calendar reminders and text messages.
3. Be sure to turn off email and instant messaging notifications. These alerts *feel* critical, which makes them all the more insidious, but the truth is that most of us can live without them. Try leaving just one way for people to interrupt you with time-sensitive things (text messages, for example).
4. Whenever a new app asks "Is it okay to show notifications?" choose "No."
5. Give it forty-eight hours or a week. See how you feel.

---

6 In case it didn't come through, we're being sarcastic.

By turning off your notifications, you'll teach your phone some manners. You'll transform it from a nonstop blabbering loudmouth into a polite bearer of important news—the kind of friend you'd actually want in your life.

20. Clear Your Homescreen

Your phone is designed for speed. Scan your face or fingerprint and you're in. And most people keep their favorite apps right on their homescreen for immediate access. *Scan, tap, app!* This friction-free process is great when you're getting driving directions, but when you're trying to get into Laser mode, it's an autobahn to distraction.

To slow things down, try making your homescreen blank. Move all the icons to the next screen over (and from the second screen to the third and so on). Don't leave anything behind on that first screen except a nice clean view of your beautiful background image.

A blank homescreen provides a tiny moment of quiet every time you use your phone. It's an intentional inconvenience, a small pause—a speed bump keeping distraction one step away. If you unlocked your phone reflexively, a blank homescreen offers you a moment to ask yourself, "Do I *really* want to be distracted right now?"

Jake

I like to take this a step further by having only one row of apps on each screen (see page 94). It's probably because I'm a neat freak, but the simplicity makes me feel calmer and more in control.

21. Wear a Wristwatch

In 1714, the British government offered a £20,000 prize (that's $5 million in 2018 money) to anyone who could invent a portable clock that could be used aboard ships. It took nearly fifty years and dozens of prototypes until finally, in 1761, John Harrison created the first "chronometer." It was a technological marvel that changed the world even though it was only barely portable—the clock had to be mounted in a special cabinet and stowed belowdecks for its maiden voyage across the Atlantic Ocean aboard the HMS *Deptford*.[7]

Today you can buy a portable clock—that is, a digital quartz wristwatch—for ten bucks. It's always accurate. It's lightweight and waterproof. It can wake you up after a nap or remind you to take dinner out of the oven. It's an amazing piece of technology.

---

7 Before the chronometer, ships had no way of keeping track of time—and, as a result, their east–west position—on long voyages. That historic Atlantic crossing aboard the *Deptford* was a huge success: The ship's navigator predicted landfall to within one mile.

But we like wearing watches for a very different reason: A wristwatch replaces the need to check your phone whenever you want to know the time. And if you're anything like us, a quick time check on your phone often pulls you into an Infinity Pool, especially when there's a notification on the screen. If you wear a watch, you can keep your smartphone out of sight. And when it's out of sight, it's easier to ignore.

JZ

In 2010, I bought a simple Timex off the clearance rack at a sporting-goods store to wear sailing. But once I put it on, I didn't want to take it off. This $17 watch was just so useful—better in many ways than a smartphone even—because its screen never cracked and the battery lasted basically forever.

22. Leave Devices Behind

Twice a week, our friend Chris Palmieri leaves his laptop and phone at the office and goes home device-free. Chris runs a busy consulting agency in Tokyo, but on those two evenings he can't check email. He can't even text. Until he goes to work the next day, he's cut off.

Inconvenient? Definitely. But Chris says the temporary isolation is made up for by improved focus—and sleep. On his device-free nights, he falls asleep earlier (11:30 p.m. instead of 1:00 a.m.), sleeps more deeply, and rarely wakes up in the middle of the night. He even remembers his dreams in the morning . . . which we assume is a good thing.

Leaving your devices behind is a helpful tactic when you want to make time for an "offline" Highlight like reading to your kids or working on a project with your hands. But if leaving your phone at work sounds terrifying (or if you have a legitimate need to use it, like for emergency contact), you can apply the underlying principle of device separation with less extreme methods. Instead of keeping your phone by your side when you get home, put it in a drawer or on a shelf; better still, stow it in your bag and shut your bag in the closet.

JZ

When I'm out and about, I usually carry my phone in my bag. And when I get home, I put my bag on a shelf and go about my life. Sometimes I forget about my phone for hours. It's a small daily reminder that life goes on without my smartphone.

Stay Out of Infinity Pools

23. Skip the Morning Check-In

24. Block Distraction Kryptonite

25. Ignore the News

26. Put Your Toys Away

27. Fly Without Wi-Fi

28. Put a Timer on the Internet

29. Cancel the Internet

30. Watch Out for Time Craters

31. Trade Fake Wins for Real Wins

32. Turn Distractions into Tools

33. Become a Fair-Weather Fan

23. Skip the Morning Check-In

When you wake up in the morning, whether you slept for five hours or ten, you've had a nice long break from the Busy Bandwagon and the Infinity Pools. This is a golden moment. The day is fresh, your brain is rested, and *you have no reason to feel distracted yet.* No news items to stress about, no work emails to stew over.

Savor it. Don't reach for email, Twitter, Facebook, or the news right away. It's very tempting to do a check-in first thing in the morning and get the latest updates; after all, *something* in the world always changes overnight. But as soon as you fire up that screen, you start a tug-of-war of attention between the present moment and everything out there on the Internet.

Put it off. The longer you postpone the morning check-in—until 9 a.m., 10 a.m., or even after lunch—the longer you preserve that feeling of rested calm and the easier it is to get into Laser mode.

JZ

Skipping the morning check-in is essential to my morning routine (described in tactic #14). The morning is prime time for my Highlight, which usually involves the computer. So each night I do myself a favor by closing all my browser tabs (#26) and logging out of Twitter and Facebook (#18). Then, after I wake up and make coffee, I'm ready to start my Highlight without any distractions from the morning check-in.

24. Block Distraction Kryptonite

Most of us have one especially powerful Infinity Pool we just can't resist. We call it "distraction Kryptonite." Just as regular Kryptonite overwhelms Superman, distraction Kryptonite gets past our defenses and sabotages our plans. Your distraction Kryptonite might be something common and obvious such as Facebook, or if you're an oddball like JZ, it might be some obscure Yahoo Group for sailboat nerds. Here's a simple litmus test: If after spending a few minutes (or, more likely, a few minutes that become an hour) with this website or app you feel regret, it's probably Kryptonite.

There are a number of ways to block Kryptonite, depending on how serious you want to get and how serious your addiction is. If your Kryptonite is a social network, email, or anything that requires a password, logging out might be enough to slow you down (#18). If your Kryptonite is a specific website, you can block it or turn off the Internet altogether during your Laser time (#28). To step it up, you can remove the app or account or browser from your smartphone (#17).

A reader named Francis told us about the experience of blocking his Kryptonite, *Hacker News*, a website packed with stories about tech startups. When he went cold turkey, Francis said, he missed the interesting articles and intelligent discussion on the site's comment boards. But the reward was a surprising boost to his emotional well-being: "I'm no longer refreshing the site forty times a day and comparing myself to a highlight reel of startup exits."

A reader named Harriette had a more extreme story. Harriette's Kryptonite was Facebook, and for her it was more than a distraction—it was an unhealthy addiction. "I was glued to my phone in a constant state of anxiety, compelled to respond to every message. My cubicle is open to view, and I had stopped even trying to emulate the appearance of working."

Harriette realized she couldn't keep this up—Facebook had taken over her life. So she decided to give it up for a week and removed it from all her devices. It was challenging, of course, but when the week was over, she didn't want to go back. "The thought of returning to social media repulsed me, so I decided to go another week without. Two weeks became two months and now ten months."

Admittedly, giving up Facebook was not without drawbacks. Many of her friends coordinated get-togethers on Facebook and wouldn't make an exception. "I was completely out of the loop. I only have contact with these longtime friends when I initiate plans—only a handful of times in the last few months."

But still, she didn't go back. "Despite the consequences, I am so much happier now. Dramatically, drastically happier. When I 'hit bottom,' I felt like I had lost control of my own brain. There is no social media meme or planning convenience that can compete with the feeling of having my mind back."

Harriette found that although some friendships fizzled without Facebook, others got stronger. The people who really wanted to spend time with her—or who she really wanted to see—found ways to contact her by phone, email, or text. "I'm not exactly incommunicado," says Harriette. "But I'm not going back to the Infinity Pool any time soon."

Harriette's experience with Facebook is certainly an extreme example, but we've heard countless similar stories. When you step away from your distraction Kryptonite, there can be a real feeling of catharsis—of joy, relief, and freedom. We fear being out of the loop, but once we're out there, we realize it's actually kind of nice.

25. Ignore the News

I can gather all the news I need on the weather report.
—PAUL SIMON, "THE ONLY LIVING BOY IN NEW YORK"

The whole concept of breaking news runs on a very potent myth: You need to know what's going on around the world, and you need to know *now*. Smart people follow the news. Responsible people follow the news. Grown-ups follow the news. Don't they?

We've got some breaking news of our own: You don't need to follow the daily news. True breaking news will find you, and the rest isn't urgent or just doesn't matter.

To see what we mean, check out today's newspaper. Or go to your favorite news website. Look at the top headlines and think critically about each one. Will that headline change any decisions you make today? How many of those headlines will become obsolete by tomorrow, next week, or next month?

How many of those headlines are designed to provoke anxiety? "If it bleeds, it leads" is a newsroom cliché, but it's true. Most news is bad news, and none of us can shrug off the nonstop bombardment of stories about conflict, corruption, crime, and human suffering without it taking a toll on our mood and our ability to focus. Even once-a-day news is a persistent, anxiety-provoking, outrage-inciting distraction.

We're not saying you have to cut yourself off completely. Instead, we suggest reading the news weekly. Anything less frequent is likely to make you feel like you're at sea, unmoored from human civilization. Anything more frequent and you'll feel fogged in, able to focus only on what's in front of you. That fog can easily obscure the important activities and people you want to prioritize.

JZ has been using the once-a-week news strategy since 2015. He prefers *The Economist*, a weekly magazine that summarizes the major events in sixty to eighty information-packed pages, but you might consider another weekly such as *TIME*, or you could subscribe to the Sunday paper. You might even schedule a time every week to sit down and browse your favorite news websites. Whichever you choose, the important thing is to disconnect from the 24/7 breaking news cycle. It can be a tough distraction to shake, but it's also a big opportunity to make time (and preserve emotional energy) for what really matters in your daily life.

JZ

I used to feel guilty if I wasn't reading the news every day. After a lot of consideration, I realized that there are three categories of things I want to know about. First, I want to be aware of major trends in economics, politics, business, and science. Second and maybe selfishly, I care about topics that will affect me directly, such as a change in health-care policy. Third, I want to know about opportunities to support others—for example, after a natural disaster. Then I realized I don't need the *daily* news for any of this. Between reading *The Economist*, listening to a weekly news podcast with my wife, and hearing the everyday talk of the town, I'm more than up to speed. Then, when I need to take action, I can always research more.

26. Put Your Toys Away

> Your real life begins after putting your house in order.
>
> —MARIE KONDO

Picture this: You're ready to work on your Highlight. Maybe it's a short story you've wanted to write or a proposal you need to get done for work. So you grab your laptop, flip open the screen, type in your password, and . . .

"LOOK AT ME! LOOK AT ME! LOOK AT ME!" Every browser tab screams at you. Your email automatically refreshes to show a dozen new messages. Facebook, Twitter, CNN . . . headlines flash, notifications pop up all over the place. You can't start on your Highlight just yet—you've got to tend to those tabs first and see what's new.

Now picture this: You grab your laptop, flip open the screen, and then . . . you see a beautiful photograph on your desktop and nothing else. No messages. No browser tabs. You signed out of email and chat at the end of the day yesterday, confident that if something urgent came up overnight, someone would call or text you. The silence is blissful. You're ready to rock.

Reacting to what's in front of you is always easier than doing what you intend. And when they're staring you right in the face, tasks such as checking email, responding to a chat, and reading the news *feel* urgent and important—but they rarely are. If you want to get into Laser mode faster, we recommend putting your toys away.

That means signing out of apps like Twitter and Facebook, closing extra tabs, and turning off email and chat at the end of each day. Like a well-behaved kid, clean up after yourself when you're done. Take it a step further and hide the bookmarks bar in your browser (we know you've got a couple of Infinity Pools in there) and configure your browser settings so that your homepage is something unobtrusive (like a clock) rather than something noisy (like a collection of sites you visit frequently).

Think of the two minutes it takes to straighten up after yourself as a small investment in your future ability to be proactive—not reactive—with your time.

27. Fly Without Wi-Fi

Because you're literally buckled into a chair,
I've always found planes a terrific spot to do a lot of
writing and reading and drawing and thinking.
—AUSTIN KLEON

One of our favorite things about airplanes (apart from the sheer wonder of flying through the air) is the enforced focus. During a flight, there's nowhere to go and nothing to do, and even if there were, the seat belt sign requires you to keep your butt in your chair. The strange parallel universe of an airplane cabin can be the perfect opportunity to read, write, knit, think, or just be bored—in a good way.

But even on an airplane, you have to change a couple of defaults to make time. First, if your seat has a screen, turn it off when you sit down. Second, if your airplane has Wi-Fi, don't pay for it. Make these two choices at the beginning of your flight, fasten your safety belt, and enjoy Laser mode at 35,000 feet.[8]

Jake

During my decade at Google, I traveled a lot, but I made a commitment to myself not to do any work in the air. I decided airplane time was my time, and I dedicated it to writing. In ten years, I wrote a lot of adventure fiction in the air, and that was hugely satisfying. And my coworkers never complained that I was offline. Maybe they figured some satellite glitch or chatty seat mate was tripping me up. Or maybe, like me, they understood the magic of being offline in flight.

28. Put a Timer on the Internet

When we were growing up, we had to dial up the Internet over a phone line (crazy, right?). Download speeds were slow, and we paid by the hour. It was a total pain in the ass.

But dial-up had one big advantage: It forced us to be intentional.

---

8   This tactic assumes that you're not traveling with children. If you've got kids with you, good luck—you may need all the distractions you can get.

If we were going to all the hassle of getting online, we'd better have a good idea of what we were going to do when we got there. When we finally dialed in, we'd have to stay on task to avoid wasting money.

Today's always-on, superfast Internet is a wonderful thing, but it's also the world's biggest Infinity Pool. It can be hard to stay in Laser mode when you know the endless possibilities of the Internet are just milliseconds away.

But the Internet doesn't *have* to be on all the time. That's just the default. When it's time to get into Laser mode, try turning the Internet off. The simplest methods are switching off the Wi-Fi on your laptop and putting your phone in airplane mode. But those methods are also simple to *undo*. It's much more effective to lock yourself out.

There are many software tools for temporarily blocking the Internet. You can find browser extensions and other apps to limit your time on specific sites or to disable everything for a predetermined length of time. New versions of these tools come out all the time; you can find our favorites on maketimebook.com.

Or you can cut off your Wi-Fi at the source. Just plug your Internet router into a simple vacation timer (the kind you use to trick would-be thieves by turning on the lights when you're out of town) and set it to click off at 6 a.m., 9 p.m., or whatever time you want to get into Laser mode to work on your Highlight.

Or you could buy a used DeLorean, build a flux capacitor, acquire some plutonium, and travel back to the year 1994 to enjoy pure dial-up. But trust us, the vacation timer is way easier.

Jake

Back on page 73, I described how I make time for my Highlight late at night. That was when I did most of my writing on *Sprint* and my adventure novel. And I never could have done it without my vacation timer.

Every time I sat down to write in the evenings, I'd get distracted by the Internet. For me, the primary culprits are sports news and email. *Should I start writing . . . or should I quickly check for Seahawks news? Should I revise that paragraph? Ugh, that's hard . . . instead, I'll open my inbox . . . hmm, new notification from LinkedIn . . . I'll archive that . . . Click!*

Click by click, I lost the will and the time to write. After two hours passed by in a blur, I'd go to bed, dejected because I'd stayed up late for nothing. I finally realized that if I was going to get things done at night, I had to either get better self-control (not happening) or shut off the Internet. With that in mind, I bought a $10 vacation timer, set it to turn off at 9:30 p.m., and plugged my Internet router into it.

Holy smokes. At 9:30 p.m., the kids were asleep and the household chores were done. The timer clicked. And . . . just like that, there was no inbox and no Seahawks. No Netflix, no Twitter, no MacRumors. My laptop turned into a desert island, and my God, it was beautiful.

29. Cancel the Internet

A reader named Chryssa sent us an extreme tactic for getting into Laser mode: She doesn't have home Internet service *at all*. That's right—no Internet. Yeah. Wow. And Chryssa's results speak for themselves. In the year since she first shared the tactic with us, she used her undistracted time to write fiction, design a new kind of pill bottle, and invent a line of toys. She's focused and prolific.

Canceling your Internet is not *quite* as extreme as it sounds, because you can still get online by using your phone as a hotspot. But that's slow-ish and expensive-ish and a big hassle. As Chryssa puts it, "That requires me to tinker with settings on two devices, and that small deterrent is enough to leave it off 99 percent of the time."

Intrigued but not quite ready to cancel your service altogether? To try this tactic without complete commitment, ask a brave friend to change your Wi-Fi password and keep it secret from you for twenty-four hours.

30. Watch Out for Time Craters

When Jake was a kid, his family took a road trip to a place called Meteor Crater, Arizona. Meteor Crater is not just a cool name; it's a real meteor crater in the middle of the desert. Tens of thousands of years ago, a 150-foot-wide chunk of rock smashed into the earth's surface, blasting a crater about a mile in diameter. A young Jake stood on the blistered rock and imagined the awesome force of impact. The crater is thirty times the size of the meteor! It's crazy to think about such a small object making such a big hole.

Or maybe it's not so crazy. After all, the same thing happens in our daily lives. Small distractions create much larger holes in our day. We call these holes "time craters," and they work like this:

- Jake posts a tweet. (90 seconds)
- Over the next two hours, Jake returns to Twitter four times to see how his tweet is doing. Each time, he skims the newsfeed. Twice he reads an article somebody shared. (26 minutes)
- Jake's tweet gets a few retweets, which feels good, so he begins mentally composing his next tweet. (Two minutes here, three minutes there, and so on)
- Jake posts another tweet, and the cycle begins all over again.

A tiny tweet can easily smash a thirty-minute crater in your day, and that's without switching costs. Each time Jake leaves Twitter and returns to his Highlight, he has to reload all the context into his brain before he's back in Laser mode.[9] So that time crater might actually be forty-five minutes, an hour, or even more.

But it's not just Infinity Pools that create time craters. There's also recovery time. A "quick" fifteen-minute burrito lunch might cost an extra three hours of food coma. A late night watching TV might cost you an hour of sleeping in and a whole day of low energy. And there's anticipation. When you don't start your Highlight because you've got a meeting coming up in thirty minutes, that's a time crater, too.

Where are the time craters in your life? That's up to you to figure out. You can't avoid them all, but you can definitely dodge some of them, and every time you do, you'll make time.

---

9   In one of our favorite studies ever, Gloria Mark of the University of California, Irvine found that it takes people twenty-three minutes and fifteen seconds to get back on task after an interruption.

31. Trade Fake Wins for Real Wins

Sharing tweets, Facebook updates, and Instagram photos can create time craters, but they're dangerous for another reason: They're fake wins.

Contributing to the conversation on the Internet feels like an accomplishment, and our brains tell us, "We've done some work!" But 99 times out of 100, these contributions are insignificant. And they come at a cost—they take up time and energy you could be using on your Highlight. Fake wins get in the way of focusing on what you really want to do.

Like time craters, fake wins come in all shapes and sizes. Updating a spreadsheet is a fake win if it helps you procrastinate on the harder but more meaningful project you chose as your Highlight. Cleaning the kitchen is a fake win if it burns up time you intended to spend with your kids. And email inboxes are a never-ending source of fake wins. Checking mail *always* feels like an accomplishment even when there's nothing new. "Good," says your brain. "I'm on top of things!"

When it's time for Laser mode, remind yourself: Your Highlight is the real win.

32. Turn Distractions into Tools

Infinity Pools like Facebook, Twitter, email, and the news are distractions, but that doesn't mean they're without value. We all started using them for a reason. Sure, at some point, a habit took hold and checking those apps became our default. But underneath the automatic routine, there's some real utility and purpose for every Infinity Pool app. The trick is to use them purposefully, not mindlessly.

When you focus on an app's purpose, you can change your relationship to it. Instead of reacting to a trigger, prompt, or interruption, you can proactively use your favorite apps—even distracting Infinity Pools—as tools. Here's how:

1. Start by identifying *why* you use a particular app. Is it purely for entertainment? Is it to keep in touch with friends and family? Is it to stay updated on certain kinds of important news? And if so, is it actually adding value to your life?

2. Next, think about how much time—per day, per week, per month—you want to spend on that activity. And consider whether this app is the best way to accomplish it. For example, you might use Facebook to keep in touch with family, but is it really the best way to do that? Would you be better off calling them?

3. Finally, consider when and how you'd like to use that app to achieve your goal. You might realize that you can read the news once a week (#25) or save email for the end of the day (#34). You might decide to give up Facebook except for sharing baby pictures. Once you decide, many of the Make Time tactics can help you put your plan into action by restricting your access at other times.

JZ

I used to spend way too much time browsing Twitter until I decided to think of it as a tool. I decided I wanted to use Twitter to spread the word about my work and respond to questions from readers. But to do that, I realized, I didn't need much time, and I didn't need to see the main feed at all. Now, I use Twitter only on my laptop—not my phone—and I limit myself to thirty minutes each day. To use that time well, I go directly to Twitter's notifications screen (by typing in the URL), skipping the distracting feed. Then, when I'm done, I log out (#18) until tomorrow's daily Twitter time.

Jake

I have less self-control than JZ, so I use a browser plug-in to limit myself to just *four* minutes per day, combined, on Twitter and news websites. This restriction has trained me to move fast. A couple of times a week, I turn off my browser plug-in and take the time to reply to the most important messages . . . and, okay, maybe read a few tweets. (As always, for our software recommendations, see maketimebook.com.)

33. Become a Fair-Weather Fan

How much time does it take to be a sports fan? Well, how much have you got? These days you can watch every game your favorite team plays in the preseason, regular season, and playoffs as well as every game *every other* team plays, all from the comfort of your living room. There is a year-round limitless supply of news, rumors, trades, draft picks, blogs, and projections. It doesn't stop. You probably could spend twenty-four hours a day staying up to date and *still* not be up to date.

Sports fandom doesn't just take time; it takes emotional energy. When your team loses, it sucks—it might bum you out and lower your energy for hours or even days.[10] Even when your team wins, the euphoria creates a time crater (#30) as you get sucked into watching highlights and reading follow-up analysis.

Sports have a powerful grip on us. They satisfy an innate tribal urge. We grow up watching local teams with our parents, families, and friends. We discuss sports with colleagues and strangers. Each game and season has an unpredictable story line, but (unlike real life) they all finish with clear-cut win-or-lose outcomes that we find deeply gratifying.

We're not asking you to give it all up. We simply suggest that you step over to the dark side by becoming a fair-weather fan. Watch games only on special occasions, like when your team is in the playoffs. Stop reading the news when they're losing. You can still love your team yet spend your time on something else.

---

10 For three months after the Seattle SuperSonics lost to the Denver Nuggets in the 1994 NBA playoffs, Jake had difficulty forming complete sentences without bursting into tears.

JZ

My grandma Katy grew up in Green Bay, Wisconsin, where her dad's high-school football coach was a man named Earl "Curly" Lambeau. NFL fans will recognize his name: The Green Bay Packers play in a stadium called Lambeau Field, and Curly himself was one of the founders of the team. Long before football's made-for-TV era, my grandma was a Packers cheerleader—on loan from the squad at Green Bay East High School, where she was a student.

So you could say that Packers fandom is in my DNA, and that makes it especially hard to be a fair-weather fan. So I take a slightly different approach: I focus on the parts of being a Packers fan that are really, really fun. For me, that means watching games with friends (preferably while eating bratwurst and drinking beer) and once every couple of years attending a freezing-cold home game at Lambeau Field.

I could spend more time following the Packers. I could read team news, analyze the key players, and keep tabs on them during the offseason. And I might enjoy football season *a little bit* more, but it would take *a lot* more time. Instead, I focus on the highlights—the parts that bring me real joy—and use the rest of my time for other things that matter.

Slow Your Inbox

We used to think an empty email inbox was the hallmark of high productivity. For years, inspired by experts like David Allen and Merlin Mann, we made it a daily goal to process every single message we received. Jake went so far as to create an email management class at Google and train hundreds of coworkers on the virtues of an empty inbox.

The empty inbox technique is based on good logic: If you clear out your messages, you won't be distracted by them while you work. Out of inbox, out of mind. And the technique works well if you get only a few emails per day. But like most office workers, we got a whole lot more than a few messages per day. Eventually, our email took on a life of its own. We were supposed to be clearing it out of the way so that we could do our work, but instead, on most days, email *was* the work.[11] It was a vicious cycle: The faster we replied, the more replies we got back and the more we strengthened the expectation of immediate responses.

As we started to make time for daily Highlights, we realized we had to stop this frenetic email processing. So for the last several years, we've been putting the brakes on our inboxes. It's not easy. But if you want to get into Laser mode and finish your Highlight, we recommend that you join us in the fight and slow down your own inbox.

The rewards go beyond Laser mode. If you check email less often, research suggests that you'll be less stressed *and* just as on top of things. A 2014 study by the University of British Columbia found that when people checked their email just three times a day (instead of as often as they wanted), they reported remarkably lower stress. As researchers Elizabeth Dunn and Kostadin Kushlev put it, "Cutting back on email might reduce stress as much as picturing yourself swimming

---

11 A 2012 study by the McKinsey Global Institute showed that office workers spend only 39 percent of their time on real work. The other 61 percent is spent communicating and coordinating. In other words, it's work about work, and email accounts for nearly half of that time. Busy Bandwagon, baby!

in the warm waters of a tropical island several times a day." Maybe more surprising, checking less often made the participants *better* at email. During the week when they checked three times a day, people answered roughly the same number of messages, but they did so 20 percent faster. Checking email less often measurably *made time*!

All that said, resetting email habits is another of those things that are easier said than done. Luckily, as two recovering email addicts, we can suggest several tactics to change your relationship with your inbox.

34. Deal with Email at the End of the Day

Instead of checking your email first thing in the morning and then getting sucked in and reacting to other people's priorities, deal with email at the end of the day. That way, you can use your prime hours for your Highlight and other important work. You'll probably have a little less energy at the end of the day, but that is actually a good thing when it comes to email: You'll be less tempted to overcommit by saying yes to every incoming request and less likely to bang out a multipage manifesto when a simple reply would do.

35. Schedule Email Time

To help establish a new end-of-day email routine, try putting it on your calendar. Yes, we want you to literally add "email time" to your calendar. When you know you've got time set aside later, it's easier to avoid wasting time on email now. And if you schedule your email time before a firm commitment such as a meeting or leaving the office, you'll get an additional boost: When email time is done, it's done. Do as much as you can in the allotted time, then move on.

36. Empty Your Inbox Once a Week

We like the clarity of an empty inbox, but we don't like the daily time commitment. JZ makes an empty email inbox a weekly goal: As long as he gets to everything by the end of the week, he's good. Give it a try. You can still skim your inbox for messages that *really* require a faster response, but respond only to those. For other urgent issues, you can ask your friends and family to contact you via text or phone. And for nonurgent ones, your colleagues (and everyone else) can learn to sit tight and wait for a reply. (See tactic #39 for tips on resetting communication expectations.)

37. Pretend Messages Are Letters

A lot of email stress comes from thinking you need to constantly check and immediately respond to every new message. But you're better off treating email like old-fashioned paper letters—you know, the kind with envelopes and stamps. Snail mail gets delivered only once a day. Most letters sit on your desk for a while before you do anything about them. And for 99 percent of communications, *that works just fine.* Try slowing down and seeing your email as what it really is: just a fancy, dressed-up, high-tech version of regular old mail.

38. Be Slow to Respond

Above all, taking control of your inbox requires a mental shift from "as fast as possible" to "as slow as you can get away with." Respond slowly to emails, chats, texts, and other messages. Let hours, days, and sometimes weeks go by before you get back to people. This may sound like a total jerk move. It's not.

In real life, you respond when people talk to you. If a colleague says, "How'd the meeting go?" you don't stare straight ahead and pretend you didn't hear. Of course not—that would be super rude. In real-life conversations, answering right away is the default. And it's a *good* default. It's respectful and helpful. But if you take the "answer right away" default into the digital world, you get in trouble.

Online, *anyone* can contact you, not just the highly relevant people in your physical vicinity. They have questions about *their* priorities— not yours—when it's convenient for *them*—not you. Every time you check your email or another message service, you're basically saying, "Does any random person need my time right now?" And if you respond right away, you're sending another signal both to them and to yourself: "I'll stop what I'm doing to put other people's priorities ahead of mine no matter who they are or what they want."

Spelled out, this sounds *insane*. But instant-response insanity is our culture's default behavior. It's the cornerstone of the Busy Bandwagon.

You can change this absurd default. You can check your inbox rarely and let messages pile up till you get around to answering them in a batch (#4). You can respond slowly to make more time for Laser mode, and if you're worried about coming off like a jerk, remind yourself that being focused and present will make you *more* valuable as a colleague and friend, not less.

The Busy Bandwagon's immediate-reply culture is powerful, and you need faith to overcome it and change your mindset. Believe in your Highlight: It *is* worth prioritizing over random disruption. Believe in Laser mode: You *will* accomplish more with a singular focus than by ricocheting through your inbox. And believe in other people: If their thing is really and truly urgent and important, they *will* track you down in person or on the phone.

39. Reset Expectations

Of course, when you limit your email time or increase your response time, you may need to manage the expectations of your colleagues and others. You could say something like this:

> *"I'm slow to respond because I need to prioritize some important projects, but if your message is urgent, send me a text."*

This message can be conveyed in person, via email, or even as an autoresponse or signature.[12] The wording is carefully designed. The justification "I need to prioritize some important projects" is eminently reasonable *and* sufficiently vague. The offer to respond to text messages provides an in-case-of-emergency plan, but because the threshold for texting or calling is higher than it is with chat and email, you'll probably be interrupted much less often.[13]

You may not even need an explicit message; your behavior can speak for itself. For example, at Google Ventures, everyone knew that

---

12 Props to Tim Ferriss, whose brass-knuckles approach to workplace interactions in *The 4-Hour Workweek* introduced us to these ideas.

13 The word *because* is powerful on its own. In a 1978 study, Harvard researchers experimented with cutting in line for the photocopy machine (remember, it was 1978). When they said, "May I use the Xerox machine?" people let them cut in 60 percent of the time. But when they said, "May I use the Xerox machine because I have to make copies?" they were let in 93 percent of the time. That's crazy! Everyone had to make copies; that's all you can do with a copier. *Because* is a magic word.

the two of us didn't respond to email quickly. If they needed something faster, they'd text us or find us in the office. But we never issued a memo about our policy. We were just slow, and people figured it out. That gave us more time for our design sprints and more time to write. In other words, more time for Laser mode and more time for our Highlights.

Some work—such as sales and customer support—really does require fast responses. But in most jobs, any reputational damage you might suffer by being slow (probably less than you think) will be more than compensated for by the increase in time for your most meaningful work.

40. Set Up Send-Only Email

Although not *receiving* email on your phone is wonderful, sometimes it's still useful to have the ability to *send* email. Good news: You can have your cake and eat it, too.

JZ

In 2014, when I decided to try a distraction-free iPhone, I was surprised at how much I missed the ability to send email. I guess I hadn't realized just how often I would send myself a quick note or reminder or use email to share files or photos with other people. I asked on Twitter whether a "send-only email" iPhone app existed. People made fun of me.

So I asked my friend Taylor Hughes (a software engineer) about it, and he helped me figure out this simple technique:

1. Create an email account to be used for outgoing email only. You can set it up anywhere, but using one of the popular webmail services makes it easy to add to your phone.

2. Set up email forwarding so that any replies to the new account will instantly go to your normal account, leaving the new account's inbox perpetually empty.

3. Add the new account to your phone instead of your regular account.

Taylor's solution worked beautifully. A few months later, my friend Rizwan Sattar (another software engineer) got intrigued by the idea of send-only email and built an iPhone app called Compose. Then, when I switched to Android, I found several send-only email apps, even a few that don't require creating a new account at all. You can find our latest app recommendations on maketimebook.com.

41. Vacation Off the Grid

Have you ever received an "out of office" email response like this?

> *"I'm on vacation this week, off the grid without access to email,
> but I'll reply to your message when I return."*

The sentence conjures the image of some remote adventure: a desolate desert landscape, a frozen forest in the Yukon, or perhaps some spelunking. But it doesn't actually *say* the person is in an isolated location with no cell towers. It just says she or he isn't accessing the Internet for a week.

You can say the exact same thing when you go on vacation, no matter where you're going. You can *choose* to go off the grid. It can be hard, because most workplaces have an implicit (and crazy) expectation that you'll check email during your time off. But even if it's hard, it is usually possible.

And it's worth the effort. Laser mode matters when you're on vacation. More, maybe, because vacation time is so limited and precious. It's the perfect time to delete your work email app (#24) and leave your laptop behind (#22). You can—and should—go off the grid anywhere and take a real vacation.

42. Lock Yourself Out

For some (cough, cough, *Jake*) email is simply irresistible. You might look at these strategies and *want* to implement them but find you don't have the willpower. But there's still hope: You can lock yourself out of your inbox.

Jake

Even after all these years and even though I know better, I'm still hopelessly in love with email. I still check it whenever possible to see if there's something new and exciting in my inbox. I am helpless to resist.

Yes, I have zero willpower. But I'm also super strict about limiting my email use. My secret is an app called Freedom. With Freedom, I can schedule times to lock myself out of email. It's how I apply the Design Your Day tactic (#13); it helps me make a plan for how I want to spend my time, then forces me to stick to that plan instead of improvising.

To create the perfect email schedule, I asked myself a few questions:

Q. In the morning, what's the absolute latest I can get away with checking email?
A. At 10:30 a.m. Since I work with people in Europe, if I check any later than 10:30 a.m., I might miss a whole day before getting back to them.

Q. How long do I need for my first email check?

A. Thirty minutes. Any more than that and I'll get seriously distracted, but any less and I might not have time to respond to an urgent and important email.

Q. What's the absolute latest I can do my second email check each day?

A. At 3 p.m. This gives me time to get back to people in the United States. More important, it gives me plenty of time to focus on other things in the early afternoon.

After doing this exercise, I set up Freedom to lock me out of everything on the Internet until 10:30 a.m. Then I have thirty minutes to check email before Freedom locks me out again—this time just from email—from 11 a.m. till 3 p.m. By that point, I've usually completed my Highlight, and it still leaves me enough time to respond to emails before the end of the day.

The great thing is that I don't have to make the hard decision to follow this schedule every day. I just changed my default once and let the app exert willpower on my behalf.

If you struggle with email love/addiction the way I do, create a schedule and then lock yourself out. In fact, you can do the same thing for any Infinity Pool. (See maketimebook .com for our latest lock-out software recommendations.)

Make TV a "Sometimes Treat"

> The most corrosive piece of technology
> that I've ever seen is called television—but then, again,
> television, at its best, is magnificent.
>
> —STEVE JOBS

TV, we love you. You give us the experience of traveling through time and space to experience other people's lives. And when our brains are totally exhausted, you help us relax and recharge. But this step in Make Time is about taking control of our attention. Remember that statistic back on page 85? Americans watch 4.3 hours of television every day—*4.3 hours per day!* That number is astonishing. Sorry, TV, but we've gotta say it: **You take too much damn time.**

As we see it, all that TV time is a gold mine: a large pile of perfectly good hours just lying there, ready to be reclaimed. As usual, all you have to do is change your default.

You don't have to throw away your television. But instead of watching every day, make it a special occasion. Or, to borrow from a phrase Jake and his wife use with their kids to explain why they don't eat ice cream every day, make it a *sometimes treat.*

This change isn't easy. Everyday television is a powerful default, and if your viewing habits are stuck on automatic pilot, you're not alone. Most living rooms are organized around a television. Our evenings often are planned around television time. And at work, TV discussion is the default small talk. We all grew up with television, so we don't always notice how much space it takes up in our lives.

But if you buck these cultural norms, you can unlock a lot of hours. Heck, even cutting down to one hour or less per day might make a huge difference. And it's not just time—you can also unlock creative energy to use for your Highlight. As Jake found with his fiction-writing projects, if you're constantly exposed to other people's ideas, it can be tough to think up your own.

Here are some experiments you can try for taking control of TV.

43. Don't Watch the News

If you make only one change to your viewing habits, cut the news. TV news is incredibly inefficient; it's an endless loop of talking heads, repetitive stories, advertisements, and empty sound bites. Rather than summarizing the most important events of the day, most TV news offers up anxiety-provoking stories handpicked to keep you agitated and tuned in. Instead, make a habit of reading the news once per day or even once per week (see #25).

44. Put Your TV in the Corner

Living rooms often are arranged around the television to make watching the default activity. Like this:

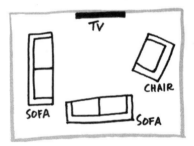

Instead, rearrange the furniture so that looking at the television is a bit awkward and inconvenient. This way, the default activity becomes conversation. Like this:

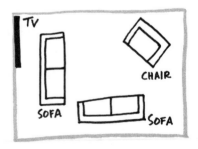

This idea comes from Jake's friends Cindy and Steve, who are the parents of three boys. "We still can and do watch shows together," Cindy says, "but the new arrangement makes it much easier to talk. And that black rectangle isn't sucking all the light out of the room." Cindy's got a good point: A turned-off screen just begs to be turned on. If you tuck it out of sight, you'll probably find it much easier to resist.

45. Ditch Your TV for a Projector

Next time you're in the market for a television, consider buying a projector and a fold-up projection screen instead. It's a cheaper way to get a big cinemalike display. It's also a pain in the ass to set up every time you want to watch. This hassle is, of course, a good thing, because it switches the default to off. You'll want to bring out the projector only for special occasions. And when you do, the viewing experience will be giant and awesome! It's the best of both worlds: a great viewing experience sometimes and more free time the rest of the time.

46. Go à la Carte Instead of All-You-Can-Eat

The trouble with streaming subscriptions is that there's *always* something on. It's like having an all-you-can-eat buffet of distraction in your living room at all times. Try canceling cable, Netflix, HBO, Hulu, and the like, and instead rent or buy movies and episodes one at a time.[14] The idea is to change your default from "let's see what's on" to "do I *really* want to watch something?" It sounds drastic, but it can

---

14 You can have Netflix à la carte, too. It's not an advertised option, but you can just wait for a show you *really* want to see (e.g., *Stranger Things*) and then subscribe for a month and immediately cancel after you've watched it. When your paid month is over, the service will turn off automatically—and you will have changed the default from permanent to temporary.

be a temporary experiment. If you want to go back, they make it *very easy* to sign up again.

47. If You Love Something, Set It Free

You don't have to give up television, but if you find it hard to reduce your hours, you might want to get extreme and try going cold turkey for a month. Unplug the TV, put it in the closet, or take it to a storage locker ten miles away and hide the key. Do whatever you have to do—just go without for a month. When the month is up, think about everything you did with that extra time and decide how much of it you want to give back to your TV.

Jake

I changed my TV habits accidentally, when my family and I moved to Switzerland in 2008. We decided to leave our old set behind, and ended up spending eighteen months without television. We weren't completely cut off from civilization: A couple of times a week we'd pay 99 cents to download an episode of *The Colbert Report* and huddle around the computer. But most of the time there was simply nothing to watch.

I grew up with TV and couldn't remember a time when it wasn't a part of my daily life. So I was surprised to find that I didn't miss it at all. There was always something to do: eat dinner as a family, play with LEGO bricks with our son, go for a walk, or read. If we really wanted to watch a movie, we could dig out a DVD and play it on the computer. We did that from time to time, but those became special occasions rather than an everyday thing.

When we came back to the United States, it took a while before we realized we no longer had a TV! And once we did remember, we were hesitant to bring it back into our lives. We'd grown accustomed to having the extra time for other activities. We knew that if we got a TV again, we'd be switching the default back to "on."

I've had television in my life as a "sometimes treat" for nearly a decade now, and it's been pretty great. I still love watching movies and the occasional series, but I feel more in control of when I do it. And I've been able to spend that gold mine of extra time on writing and hanging out with my sons. Just like ice cream, TV is so much more satisfying when I have it occasionally instead of a huge serving every day.

Find Flow

48. Shut the Door

> The closed door is your way of telling the world and
> yourself that you mean business.
>
> —STEPHEN KING, *ON WRITING*

Steve's right. If your Highlight requires focused work, do yourself a favor and shut the door. If you don't have a room with a door, look for one you can camp out in for a few hours. And if you can't find one, put on headphones—even if you don't actually put on any music.

Headphones and closed doors signal to everyone else that you shouldn't be interrupted, and they send a signal to you, too. You're telling yourself, "Everything I need to pay attention to is right here." You're telling yourself it's time for Laser mode.

49. Invent a Deadline

Nothing's better for focus than a deadline. When someone else is waiting expectantly for results, it's a *lot* easier to get into Laser mode.

The trouble is that deadlines are usually for things we dread (like doing taxes), not for things we *want* to do (like practicing the ukulele). But this is an easy problem to solve. You can invent a deadline.

Invented deadlines are the secret ingredient in our design sprints. The team schedules customer interviews on Friday of every sprint week so that starting on Monday, everyone knows the clock is ticking. They *have* to solve their challenge and build a prototype before Thursday night; after all, those strangers are showing up on Friday! The deadline is totally made up, but it helps teams stay in Laser mode for five straight days.

You, too, can create a deadline that will help you make time for something you want to do. Register for a 5K run. Invite your friends over for a homemade pasta dinner before you've learned how to make it. Sign up to exhibit at an art show before you've painted the pictures. Or you can simply tell a friend what your Highlight is today and ask them to hold you accountable for getting it done.

JZ

I ran track and cross-country in high school, but during four years of college, I didn't manage to get out for even *one* jog around campus. (I was busy for sure, but I think it had more to do with the pizza-and-beer lifestyle I was living back then.) So by the time I graduated and moved to Chicago, I was looking for a way to get back into distance running. I just couldn't seem to make the time.

That first summer, my friend Matt Shobe asked if I wanted to run the Bastille Day 5K in Chicago. My first reaction was "No way, I'm not ready," but then I realized that Bastille Day was more than a month away. I had enough time to train, and I *was* looking for an excuse to get running. Hell yeah, I'd do it! That commitment was all the motivation I needed.

With an invented deadline, I put myself on a simple training plan and got to work. It turned out that making time to train wasn't that hard, the race was fun, and I even managed to finish in under twenty minutes. I've been a big fan of invented deadlines ever since.

50. Explode Your Highlight

When you're not sure where to start, try breaking your Highlight into a list of small, easy-to-do bits. For example, if your Highlight is "Plan vacation," you can explode it into bits like these:

- Check calendar for vacation dates.
- Skim guidebook and make list of possible destinations.
- Discuss destinations with family and choose favorite.
- Research airfare online.

Note that each item includes a verb. Each one is specific. And each one is small and relatively easy. We learned this technique from productivity shaman David Allen, who has this to say about breaking projects into physical actions:

Shifting your focus to something that your mind perceives as a doable, completable task will create a real increase in positive energy, direction, and motivation.

In the vocabulary of Make Time, tiny doable to-dos help you build momentum and lock into Laser mode. So if your Highlight feels overwhelming, add a little dynamite.

51. Play a Laser Sound Track

If you're struggling to get into Laser mode, try a cue.

A cue is any trigger that causes you to act consciously or unconsciously. It's the first step in the "habit loop" Charles Duhigg describes in *The Power of Habit:* First, a **cue** prompts your brain to start the loop. The cue triggers you to perform a **routine** behavior without thinking, on autopilot. Finally, you get a **reward:** some result that makes your brain feel good and encourages it to run the same routine again the next time you encounter the cue.

Many cues exist in our environment and trigger not-so-great behaviors, such as the smell of French fries that lures us into double cheeseburger debauchery. But you can create your own cue to help kick off a *good* habit, like Laser mode.

We suggest using music as your cue for Laser mode. Try playing the same song or album every time you start your Highlight, or choose a specific song or album for each type of Highlight. For example, when Jake starts a super short workout (#64), he plays Michael Jackson's "Billie Jean" and "Beat It." Every time he works on his adventure novel, he plays the album *Hurry Up, We're Dreaming* by M83.[15] And whenever he sits down to play trains with his younger son, he puts on *Currents* by Tame Impala. After a few songs, he's in the zone. The music reminds his brain which routine to run.

He doesn't play the songs at other times—they're reserved for these special activities. So after a few repetitions, the music becomes part of the habit loop, cuing his brain to get into a distinct version of Laser mode.

To find your own sound track, think of a song you really like but don't listen to all that often. Once you choose your sound track, make a commitment to yourself that you'll listen to it only when you want to enter Laser mode. Make sure your Laser sound track is something you love to hear; that way, listening to it becomes both a cue *and* a reward.

For those about to rock, we salute you.

---

15 When writing nonfiction, he plays *Master of Puppets* by Metallica, but he's too embarrassed to admit it.

52. Set a Visible Timer

Time is invisible. But it doesn't have to be.

We'd like to introduce you to the Time Timer. And we should say up front that we don't get a cut of Time Timer sales, because this will sound like a blatant sales pitch.

Quite simply, we love the Time Timer (and we love saying "Time Timer"). We use Time Timers in every one of our design sprints. Jake has five Time Timers at home. The Time Timer is amazing.

The Time Timer is a special clock designed for children. You set an interval from one to sixty minutes, and a red disk slowly disappears as time elapses. When it gets to zero, the timer beeps. It's very simple. It's pure genius—it makes time *visible*.

If you use the Time Timer when you're getting into Laser mode, you'll feel an instant, visceral sense of urgency in a totally good way. By showing you that time is elapsing, the Time Timer will get you to focus on the task at hand.

Jake

I often set a Time Timer when I'm playing with my younger son. I know this sounds horrible—judge me if you must—but it makes it clear to him how much time we have and reminds me that this time is precious and fleeting and I should go all in and enjoy the moment.

53. Avoid the Lure of Fancy Tools

What's the best to-do-list app? The most exquisite notepad and pen for taking notes and sketching? The finest smartwatch?

Everyone has their favorites. The Internet is home to many a treatise about the Best This or the Cool New Way to Do That.[16] But this obsession with tools is misguided. Unless you're a carpenter, a mechanic, or a surgeon, choosing the perfect tool is usually a distraction, yet another way to stay busy instead of doing the work you want to be doing.

It's easier to set up fancy writing software on your laptop than to actually write the screenplay you've been dreaming of. It's easier to buy Japanese notepads and Italian pens than to actually start sketching. And unlike checking Facebook—which everyone knows isn't productive—researching and messing with fancy tools *feels* like work. But it usually isn't.

Plus, it's easier to get into Laser mode when you adopt simple tools that are readily available. That way, when something breaks, or your battery dies, or you forget your gadget at home, you won't miss a beat.

---

16 In fact, discussion of gadgets, apps, tools, and gear follows only cat videos in Internet popularity. Source: our proprietary Study of Links We've Clicked.

JZ

I've been burned by fancy tools. Back in 2006, I discovered the perfect productivity software: a simple but powerful app called Mori that allowed for infinitely customizable note taking and filing.

I was elated, and spent countless hours configuring Mori on my laptop and loading all my projects into it. And I was right: It *was* perfect. Mori became an extension of my brain.

But after a few months, things started breaking down. I upgraded my computer's operating system, only to find that Mori wasn't compatible with the new version. I'd want to look at my notes at home but realize I had left my laptop at work. And then the developer shut down Mori altogether. I was distraught.

That's the other problem with fancy tools: they're fragile. Anything from a technical glitch to my own forgetfulness could keep me from getting into Laser mode and spending time on my Highlight.

After Mori vanished, I started using simple, readily available tools to manage my work: text files on my computer, notes on my phone, basic Post-its, free hotel pens, that sort of thing. More than ten years later, my everyday tools work as well as ever. And whenever I get tempted by a new fancy tool, I just remember Mori.

54. Start on Paper

In our design sprints, we found that we did better work when we turned off our laptops and used pens and paper instead. And the same is true for your personal projects.

Paper improves focus, because you can't waste time picking the perfect font or searching the Web instead of working on your Highlight. Paper is less intimidating, too—while most software is designed to guide you through a series of steps that will lead to a finished product, paper allows you to find your own way to a cohesive idea. And paper opens up possibilities, because whereas Word is designed for lines of text and PowerPoint is designed for graphs and bullet points, on paper, you can do anything at all.

Next time you're struggling to get into Laser mode, put away your computer or tablet and pick up a pen.

Stay in the Zone

Getting into Laser mode is only half the battle—you have to stay in the zone and maintain attention on your Highlight. Focus is hard work, and it's inevitable that you'll be tempted by distraction. Here are our favorite techniques for letting go of that temptation and focusing on what really matters.

55. Make a "Random Question" List

It's natural to feel twitchy for your phone or browser. You'll wonder if you have any new email.[17] You'll feel a burning desire to know *Who was that actor in that movie?*[18]

Instead of reacting to every twitch, write your questions on a piece of paper (*How much do wool socks cost on Amazon? Any Facebook updates?*). Then you can stay in Laser mode, secure in the knowledge that those pressing topics have been captured for future research.

56. Notice One Breath

Pay attention to the physical sensations of a single breath:

1. Breathe in through your nose. Notice the air filling up your chest.
2. Breathe out through your mouth. Notice your body softening.

You can repeat this if you like, but one breath really can be enough to reset your attention. Paying attention to your body shuts up the

---

17   Yes, you do.

18   It was Pierce Brosnan.

noise in your brain. And even a pause that lasts only one breath can bring your attention back to where you want it—on your Highlight.

57. Be Bored

When you're deprived of distraction, you may feel bored—but boredom is actually a good thing. Boredom gives your mind a chance to wander, and wandering often leads you to interesting places. In separate studies, researchers at Penn State and the University of Central Lancashire found that bored test subjects were better at creative problem solving than were their nonbored peers.[19] So next time you are feeling understimulated for a few minutes, just sit there. You're bored? Lucky you!

58. Be Stuck

Being stuck is a tiny bit different from being bored. When you're bored, you don't have anything to do, but when you're stuck, you know exactly what you *want* to do—your brain just isn't sure how to proceed. Maybe you don't know what to write next, or where to begin on a new project.

The easy road out of Stucksville is to do something else. Check your phone. Dash off an email. Turn on the TV. These things are easy, but they cut into the time you've made for your Highlight. Instead, just be stuck. Don't give up. **Stare at the blank screen, or switch to paper, or walk around, but keep your focus on the project at hand.** Even when your conscious mind feels frustrated, some quiet part of

---

19 In case you're wondering how the researchers bored their test subjects (we were), Penn State used boring videos and the University of Central Lancashire made people copy numbers out of a phone book. Researchers are jerks.

your brain is processing and making progress. Eventually, you *will* get unstuck, and then you'll be glad you didn't give up.

59. Take a Day Off

If you've tried these techniques and you still don't have Laser mode in you, don't beat yourself up. You might need a rest day. Energy—especially creative energy—can fluctuate, and sometimes you need time to replenish it. Most of us can't take the day off work whenever we want, but you *can* give yourself permission to take it easy. Try taking real breaks throughout the day (#80) and switching to a joyful Highlight that'll help you recharge.

60. Go All In

We believe in rest, but there is an alternative. Here's a tactic from an honest-to-goodness modern-day monk:

> *You know the antidote to exhaustion is not necessarily rest. . . .*
> *The antidote to exhaustion is wholeheartedness.*
> —BROTHER DAVID STEINDL-RAST

Okay, let's talk about this wholeheartedness idea. Wholeheartedness is complete commitment, holding nothing back. It's letting go of caution and allowing yourself to care about your work, a relationship, a project, anything. Throwing yourself into the moment with enthusiasm and sincerity.

We believe wholeheartedness is fundamental to everything this book is about: presence, attention, and making time for what matters.

And Brother David's case for wholeheartedness is a new (for us, at least) way of approaching Laser mode.

Of course, both physical rest and mental rest are extremely important. But if you're feeling worn out and unable to focus, Brother David says you don't always need to take a break. Sometimes, if you go all in and embrace the current task with wild abandon, you may find it becomes easier to focus. You may find the energy is *already there*.

This sounds like a radical idea, but we've seen it happen. We've seen teams in a design sprint get the chance to work in a wholehearted way—finally focusing on a project they really care about—and become filled with energy. And we've felt it ourselves.

Jake

This is what I experienced that evening when I deleted everything on my phone. Before, I had been splitting my attention between playing with my kids and looking at my phone. I was holding back and conserving energy. But when I went all in and threw myself wholeheartedly into assembling the wooden train track and making choo-choo noises, the tiredness went away.

JZ

I feel this every time I go sailing offshore. It can be truly exhausting—remaining alert, moving around a constantly shifting boat, sleeping in two- or three-hour shifts—but it's an experience that rewards wholeheartedness. No matter how I'm feeling, when I head out to sea, I embrace the challenge wholeheartedly. Any feelings of exhaustion, stress, or unease just fall away.

Wholeheartedness is not easy. It's especially difficult when you're reacting to Infinity Pools or the Busy Bandwagon. And if you're used to "playing it cool," it may take some practice before you can let your guard down and let yourself be enthusiastic again.

But perhaps the biggest obstacle is when your heart isn't *really* in the current task—for example, when you're working at a job that's not right for you. In fact, that's the context for Brother David's quote: He was advising a friend who was burned out at work to leave and focus on his passion. We aren't advising you to quit your job, but we are reminding you that it's important to be proactive and seek out moments when you can be passionate about your efforts. If you choose exciting ways to spend your time, being wholehearted isn't so hard.

Energize

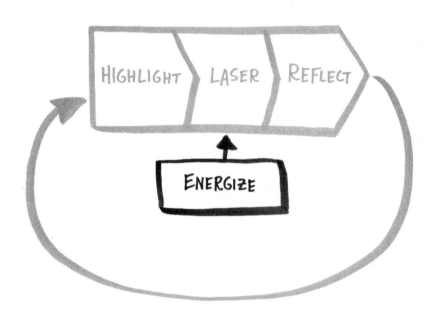

I like university professors, but you know . . .
they look upon their body as a form of
transport for their heads, don't they?
It's a way of getting their head to meetings.

—SIR KEN ROBINSON

So far in this book, we've talked about ways to make time by choosing where to focus your effort, adjusting your calendar and devices, and blocking out distractions to boost attention. But there's another, even more basic way to make time. If you can increase your energy every day, you'll turn moments that might otherwise be lost to mental and physical fatigue into usable time for your Highlights.

You Are More Than a Brain

Imagine you've got a battery inside you. All your energy is stored in the battery, and just like the battery in your phone or laptop, it can be charged all the way up to 100 percent or can drain all the way down to zero.

When your battery is empty, you're totally exhausted—you feel wrung out and maybe even depressed. This is when you're most likely to get distracted by Infinity Pools such as Facebook and email. Then you feel worse because you're tired *and* you're annoyed at yourself for wasting time. That's 0 percent. It sucks.

Now imagine how it feels when your battery is full. You've got a spring in your step. You feel well rested, your mind is sharp, and your body feels alert and alive. You're ready to take on any project—not only ready but excited. Can you visualize the feeling? Pretty nice, right? That's 100 percent.

Choosing a Highlight and getting into Laser mode are the core of Make Time. But the secret sauce is Energize. Our thesis is simple: If you have energy, it's easier to maintain your focus and priorities and avoid reacting to distractions and demands. With a full battery, you have the power to be present, think clearly, and spend your time on what matters, not default to what's right in front of you.

To get the energy you need to maintain a focused, high-performing brain, you've got to take care of your body. Of course, everyone knows our brains and bodies are connected. But these days, it's easy to feel that the brain is the only part that matters. When we sit in a conference room, drive a car, use a computer, or dink around on a phone, we're living in our brains. Oh, sure, our fingers tap buttons and our bottoms keep us on the chair. But for the most part, the body is merely a Segway scooter for the brain: an efficient but awkward form of transportation.

This perception of the brain and body as completely separate entities is established early in life and reinforced often. When the two of us were growing up (Jake in rural Washington State, JZ in rural Wisconsin), we exercised our brains in math, English, and social studies and exercised our bodies in gym class and on sports teams. Two separate worlds. The brain over here, the body over there.

In college, our brains had more to do and exercise was no longer a course requirement. When we got full-time office jobs, our brains were busier still, our calendars were fuller, and taking care of our bodies became even less convenient. And so we did what most people do: We tried every tool or trick at our disposal to become more efficient with our brains—and we put our bodies on the sideline. Two separate worlds. The brain over here, the body *way* over there.

The defaults of today's world assume that the brain is the one driving the bus, but that's not really how it works. When you don't take care of your body, your brain can't do its job. If you've ever felt sluggish and uninspired after a big lunch or invigorated and clearheaded after exercising, you know what we mean. **If you want energy for your brain, you need to take care of your body.**

But how? There are approximately a kajillion scientific studies, books, blog posts, and talk-show guests out there ready to tell you how to increase your energy. Frankly, it can be pretty confusing. Should you get more sleep or train yourself to sleep less? Is aerobic exercise best? Or strength training? And when the scientific consensus inevitably changes—like when it shifted from warning against eating fat to recommending it—what should you do?

We've spent years trying to make sense of all this advice, specifically looking for the best ways to build energy to fuel our brains in our quest to make more time. Eventually, we realized that 99 percent of what you need to know about increasing your energy is right there in human history. All you need to do is travel back in time to check it out.

You Awaken to the Roar of a Saber-Toothed Tiger

Disoriented, you rub your eyes and stretch. You're lying in the grass at the edge of a dense forest, the pale light of dawn filtering through the trees. Beside you is a note:

Hi! You've been zapped back in time 50,000 years.

Your stomach grumbles, and your head feels fuzzy. You could really go for a cappuccino and a croissant, but Italy and France won't be invented for millennia. Somewhere in the distance, another roar echoes off the hills. Today, you decide, is going to suck.

But then . . . it doesn't suck.

First, you meet a local hunter-gatherer named Urk. Urk looks like your stereotypical caveman. He wears a tunic made from a mountain lion pelt and has a beard that would put any hipster to shame.

Urk is startled when he sees you. He postures and waves his stone ax. But once he gets a good look at your absurd clothes and haircut, he realizes you pose no serious threat. Urk laughs, you smile, and the ice is broken.

HA HA HA!

Urk's manners are coarse and his mountain lion pelt could stand a good laundering, but he turns out to be a pretty cool dude. He introduces you to his tribe of hunter-gatherers, and they bring you along on a berry-picking expedition. The trek covers miles of territory, and by the time the sun sets, you're exhausted. You share a dinner of venison with the crew, and then you snuggle under a nice thick mammoth hide, stare up at the stars, and drift off to your best night's sleep in years.

Over the next few weeks, the hunter-gatherers teach you some basics: how to make a stone ax of your own, how to identify poisonous plants, and how to wave your hands to chase deer toward the spear throwers.

Every day, you walk for miles. Every day, you also have plenty of time to kick back, share a meal with the others, or spend some time alone sharpening a spear or just daydreaming. Your body grows stronger while your mind grows more relaxed. One evening, as you and the tribe make camp in a nice big cave, you're struck by inspiration. "Hey, everybody," you say. "This wall would be *awesome* for some cave paintings! Who's in?"

Of course, nobody answers, because they don't speak English. But you don't care. You always told yourself you'd learn to paint someday, and tomorrow you're gonna make time to start.

Welcome back to the twenty-first century. And don't worry, this isn't a pitch to go paleo, adopt an all-cashew diet, or jog barefoot with nothing but an elk hide shielding you from the elements. We introduced you to Urk for an important reason: We believe there's a lot to be learned—about both our bodies and our brains—from prehistoric humans. At a time when the modern world seems crazy, it's helpful to remember that *Homo sapiens* evolved to be hunter-gatherers, not screen tappers and pencil pushers.

Prehistoric humans ate a variety of foods and often waited all day (or longer) for a proper meal. Constant movement was the norm. Walking, running, and carrying were interspersed with brief bouts of more intense effort. Yet there was plenty of time for leisure and family: Anthropologists estimate that ancient humans "worked" only thirty hours a week. They lived and worked in tight-knit communities in which face-to-face communication was the only option. And of course they got plenty of sleep, going to bed when it was dark and rising with the sun.

We're the descendants of those ancient humans, but our species hasn't evolved nearly as fast as the world around us has. That means we're still wired for a lifestyle of constant movement, varied but relatively sparse diets, ample quiet, plenty of face-to-face time, and restful sleep that's aligned with the rhythm of the day.

Our modern world, nice as it is, defaults to an entirely different lifestyle. Physical activity defaults to sitting. Human interaction defaults to screens. Food comes wrapped in plastic, and sleep often is squeezed into our days as an afterthought. How the heck did we get here?

The Modern Lifestyle Is an Accident

Homo sapiens appeared in Africa around 200,000 years ago. For the next 188,000 years, everybody had the same job title—hunter-gatherer—and our days looked like Urk's days. Then, around 12,000 years ago, humans began farming, and most of us stopped our nomadic ways to settle down in villages and towns. (The name *agricultural revolution* makes it sound like a sudden stroke of genius, but the switch was probably accidental and occurred gradually over the course of several generations.) Compared with the life of a hunter-gatherer, farm work and village life sucked. Leisure time plummeted. Violence and disease skyrocketed. Unfortunately, there was no going back.[1]

We kept moving forward. Over the centuries, we switched from wood to fossil fuel. We mastered steam and electricity. Then, during the last couple of centuries, things went bonkers. We created factories. We developed the television and then became obsessed with it, changing our sleep schedules to fit in daily TV time. We invented the home computer, the Internet, and the smartphone. Each time, we wrapped our lives around the new invention. Each time, there was no going back.

THE LAST 200,000 YEARS:
Nothing changed, then everything changed all at once

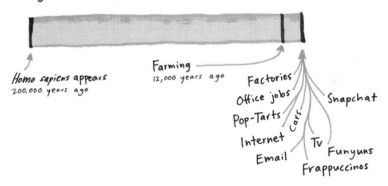

Today's world is not a utopia planned out by geniuses. It's been shaped very accidentally by the technologies that have stuck over the last few centuries, decades, and years. We're built for one world, but

---

1   Check out Yuval Noah Harari's *Sapiens* for a fascinating account of the accidental nature of the agricultural revolution and its unintended (but irreversible) consequences.

we live in another. Underneath our smartwatches, fancy haircuts, and factory-made designer jeans, we're Urk.

So how can we fuel our caveman brains and bodies with the energy we need to do modern work? In the sea of confusing, overwhelming, and sometimes contradictory advice from scientists, health gurus, and self-help authors (ahem), Urk is your beacon. By living like Urk, you go back to basics—a little bit closer to the lifestyle humans evolved for, but without losing everything that's great about our modern world.

Don't get us wrong: Prehistoric times weren't all fun and games. Urk had zero access to antibiotics or chocolate, and he brushed his teeth with a stick. But if you adopt a few small Urk-like activities, you can get the best of the twenty-first century *and* the best from your old-fashioned *Homo sapiens* self.

Act Like a Caveman to Build Energy

The whole idea of going back to basics represents a big opportunity: Because life today is so out of sync with our hunter-gatherer bodies, there's a huge margin for improvement. The highest-yield methods— that is, the ones in which the smallest shift produces the largest benefit—follow these principles:

1. Keep It Moving

Urk was constantly walking, carrying, lifting, and working. Our bodies and brains perform best when we're in motion. To charge your battery, you don't have to train for a marathon or attend predawn boot camp. Just a twenty- to thirty-minute session can make the brain work better, reduce stress, improve your mood, *and* make it easier to sleep well, providing more energy for the next day—a pretty sweet positive feedback loop. We'll suggest lots of tactics for adding more movement into your day.

2. Eat Real Food

Urk ate what he could find and catch: vegetables, fruits, nuts, and animals. Nowadays, we're surrounded by invented and manufactured foods. We won't ask you to overhaul your diet completely, but we will suggest some tactics for shifting your defaults away from fake food and toward eating like Urk.

3. Optimize Caffeine

All right, we know: Coffee shops were few and far between in prehistoric times. But while we're on the subject of your brain and body, it's crucial to talk about caffeine, because it's such an easy place to make improvements to your energy level.

4. Go Off the Grid

In Urk's world, almost nothing ever happened. Except for the occasional run-in with a mastodon, there was no breaking news. Quiet was the norm, and humans evolved to not only tolerate silence but use it for productive thought or focused work. Today's constant noise and distractions are a disaster for your energy and your attention span. We'll show you easy ways to find moments of quiet, like taking a break without screens and leaving your headphones at home.

5. Make It Personal

Urk was a social animal, interacting with friends face-to-face. Today, our interactions are mostly screen to screen, but you can kick it old school by finding the people who charge your battery and getting together in person. It's an easy paleolithic mood boost.

6. Sleep in a Cave

According to a 2016 study by the University of Michigan, Americans spend around eight hours in bed every night, as do folks in Britain, France, and Canada. But despite what seems like a decent amount of time in bed, most of us still don't get enough sleep. What the heck? Sleep quality is more important than quantity, and our world is full of barriers—from screens to schedules to caffeine—to getting good sleep. Urk's evenings followed a predictable rhythm, he slept in the dark, and he never lay awake fretting over email. We'll talk about how you can follow his lead to rest better, feel better, and think better.

Look, we get it. Advice like this—*Get more exercise! Eat healthier! Live like a caveman!*—is easy to give but hard to follow. That's why, instead of stopping at high-level philosophies, we're about to get very specific about how to put these ideas into practice one bite-size step at a time. Now let's plug in and charge that battery.

Keep It Moving

61. Exercise Every Day (but Don't Be a Hero)

What you do every day matters
more than what you do once in a while.
—GRETCHEN RUBIN

Moving your body is the best way to charge your battery. But you don't need lengthy complicated workouts. Our philosophy is simple:

Exercise for about twenty minutes . . .
Research shows that the most important cognitive, health, and mood benefits of exercise can be attained in just twenty minutes.

. . . every day . . .
The energy and mood boosts from exercise last about a day, so to feel good every day, get some exercise every day. As an added bonus, daily habits are easier to keep than sometimes habits.[2]

. . . (and give yourself partial credit).
Don't stress about perfection. If you manage to exercise only four out of seven days this week, hey, four is better than three! If you don't feel up for a twentyish-minute workout today, get out there for ten. Sometimes a ten-minute walk or run or swim will turn into twenty or

---

2   Yes, we know you need rest days. But if you aim for every day, chances are good that you'll accidentally get some rest days because of scheduling, weather, or other interruptions. And even on a rest day, you probably can take a walk.

longer because it feels so great—you won't want to stop once you start moving. Other times, it'll just be ten minutes, and that's cool, too. It's better than zero, and you still get an energy boost.[3]

Plus, the simple act of putting on your workout gear and getting out there will strengthen the habit, making it easier to motivate yourself for longer workouts in the future.

This "just enough" approach requires a mindset shift, because most of us have preconceived notions about what exercise actually is. Often, these notions are tied up in our egos. Whether we identify as basketball players, rock climbers, yogis, runners, cyclists, swimmers, or whatever, many of us have a bias toward activities we consider "real exercise." Anything less doesn't count even if the ideal "real exercise" doesn't fit our lives very well.

Modern culture encourages these unrealistic expectations about exercise. Shoe companies exhort you to do more, faster, and better. Magazine headlines scream about new methods to sculpt your abs and blast your core. People brag about running marathons by putting "26.2" stickers on their cars, and not to be outdone, ultramarathoners have "50" and "100" stickers to show those wimpy regular marathoners who's boss.

---

3   The research on light exercise and the brain is pretty amazing. For example, a 2016 study at Radboud University in the Netherlands found that exercise boosted short-term memory, even when the information being recalled was learned hours *before* the participants exercised. A 2017 University of Connecticut study found that light physical activity (such as taking a walk) boosted psychological well-being, whereas vigorous activity had no positive or negative effect. There are a seemingly endless supply of these kinds of studies. For a thorough (and thoroughly enjoyable) look at the science of what regular small-dose exercise does for your brain, read John Medina's *Brain Rules*.

How are us normal people supposed to feel? Does exercise count only if we're training for a quadruple triathlon or pulling an eighteen-wheeler by a chain clamped between our teeth? The answer is no. Wish those ultramarathoners the best, then ignore them. Go small and go every day—or as close to every day as possible.

Making the shift to daily doable exercise might mean giving up bragging rights. It might mean letting go of the ideal activity in favor of the workout you can actually do consistently. Making this mental shift is tough. We can't do it for you, but we can give you permission: It's okay to not be perfect. There is more to you than how you sweat.

Jake

I used to think of myself as a "serious basketball player." In my mind, it wasn't real exercise unless I played three hours of hoops four days a week. But with kids and a job, that amount of exercise simply wasn't sustainable. I went through bursts of full-tilt basketball in which I'd play for several hours several days in a row—exhausting myself, often injuring myself, and falling behind on work—followed by weeks or months of not doing *any* exercise and feeling terribly guilty. It was all or nothing.

I remember the moment I changed my exercise mindset. I'd just come into the office after a three-hour basketball session. I limped on a twisted ankle and collapsed at my desk, mentally and physically depleted. I had no energy left for work; it seemed like my computer mouse weighed a hundred pounds.

Then a vision flashed across my mind's eye of how I'd

felt the *previous* morning when I'd taken a ten-minute jog around the neighborhood, pushing my toddler son in a stroller so that he could get some fresh air. It was the kind of light exercise my athlete ego considered inadequate; such a short run didn't "count." Yet the day I jogged, I'd arrived at work invigorated, focused for several hours, and finished an important design project.

"My God," I thought, "I need to change my approach." Certainly, basketball was fun and a good workout. But I was going way overboard every time I played, and that was a recipe for exhaustion and injury.

Right then and there, I decided to lower my workout bar and give myself credit for any amount of exercise, no matter how small. When I couldn't (or shouldn't) play basketball—which was most days—I'd run, and when I couldn't run, heck, I'd take a walk.

My anecdotal experience matches the science. I feel better on days when I exercise a little: less stressed, more energetic, and generally happier. And unlike the heroic efforts, this right-size everyday exercise routine is sustainable. Running or walking became a real *habit*—eventually, it kind of went on autopilot. I still play basketball once in a while, but it's no longer the only exercise that counts. And by giving myself permission to do just a little every day, I'm a lot happier.

62. Pound the Pavement

We were born to walk. In the history of human evolution, the ability to walk upright actually came before our big, thinking brains. But in the modern world, we default to motorized transportation. Most of us can get wherever we need to go by car, bus, or train, and by making it so easy *not* to walk, this default robs us of a great opportunity to energize.

To put it in technical terms, walking is really, really darned good for you. Reports from Harvard and the Mayo Clinic (among others) show that walking helps you lose weight, avoid heart disease, reduce the risk of cancer, lower blood pressure, strengthen bones, and improve your mood through the release of painkilling endorphins. Walking is practically a wonder drug.

And walking helps make time you can use to think, daydream, or meditate. JZ often uses walk time to plan and think about his Highlight. Sometimes he starts drafting a new chapter, blog post, or story in his head. But there's no reason walking has to be Zen time. You can listen to podcasts or audiobooks while you walk. You can even talk on the phone. (Depending on where you walk, it might be too noisy for serious conversations, but calling Mom to say hi will work just fine.)

A daily walk doesn't have to be "one more thing to do." Try substituting walking for your usual mode of transportation. If the distance is too far, maybe you can walk part of the way. Jump off the bus or train one stop early and make the rest of the journey on foot. Next time you drive somewhere with a big parking lot, skip the search for the perfect spot and park far away. If you change the default from "ride when possible" to "walk when possible," you'll see opportunities everywhere.

Altogether, walking may be the world's simplest and most convenient form of exercise, but despite being easy, it packs a powerful charge for your battery. To paraphrase Nancy Sinatra, your feet were made for walking—and that's just what they should do.

JZ

In 2013 my office moved from the suburbs to the city, about two miles from home. I decided to start walking to work, because why not? The weather is pretty nice in San Francisco, the bus was crowded, and there was no way I was going to pay for parking downtown.

As walking became my routine, I noticed something surprising: I felt like I had *more time* when I walked to work. Technically, walking took longer than riding or driving, but it didn't feel that way, because walking created time I could use for thinking or mentally working on my Highlight.

63. Inconvenience Yourself

Okay, we know walking all over the place—as we advised you to do in the previous tactic—is pretty inconvenient. But that's on purpose. We think choosing inconvenience is a great way to find opportunities for exercise outside the gym. You just have to be willing to reset your default from "convenient" to "energizing," like this:

1. Cook Dinner

Carrying groceries, moving around the kitchen, lifting, chopping, stirring—it all requires moving your body. For some, cooking is meditative; it's a great way to make time for thinking or reflecting. For others, it's genuinely enjoyable and an excuse to spend face time with friends and family (#81). Plus, the food you'll make at home is probably healthier than restaurant food and therefore more energizing.

2. Take the Stairs

Elevators are super convenient, but they're kind of awkward, right? Which direction do you look? Should you say hi to the guy from accounting[4] or keep your eyes glued to your phone? Spare yourself these stress-inducing decisions, keep it moving, and take the stairs.

3. Use a Suitcase Without Wheels

Ditch the rolling suitcase and carry your stuff instead. Think of it as a miniature strength workout, but at the airport instead of the gym. You get the idea. There are opportunities to be inconvenienced everywhere!

Jake
Wait a second. The wheeled suitcase is the best invention since fire. I'm not giving mine up!

Of course, we should mention that we ourselves are hypocrites. We love conveniences, from delivery apps to escalators to, um, cars. We don't suggest completely rejecting the conveniences of modern life, just

---

4   No offense to accountants. We love accountants!

that you say no from time to time and make those conveniences a conscious decision rather than the default way of life.

JZ

Remember, nobody has to use every tactic. Not even us.

64. Squeeze in a Super Short Workout

Sometimes things that seem too good to be true turn out to be both good *and* true. That's why we're fans of high-intensity interval training, an approach to exercise that emphasizes quality over quantity. In high-intensity interval training—or, as we call it, a "super short workout"— you complete a series of brief but intense moves. You can choose body weight exercises such as push-ups, pull-ups, and squats. You can sprint. You can lift weights. And you can finish a proper workout in as little as five or ten minutes.

The best part is that super short workouts are truly energizing. And it's not just a time-saving substitute for "real" exercise. In fact, there's evidence that high-intensity exercise is better overall than the longer medium-intensity workouts we all think are necessary. Summarizing several new scientific studies, the *New York Times* says: "Seven minutes or so of relatively punishing training may produce greater gains than an hour or more of gentler exercise." Greater gains, in less time, for no money, with no equipment: It really does sound too good to be true.

This too-good-to-be-true workout makes sense in the context of Urk's world. You can easily imagine him lifting, pushing, climbing, and pulling as he returns from a successful hunting trip or scales a peak to get a better view. A super short workout shouldn't be the only exercise you get—but it is a fast, convenient way to charge your battery.

If you want to give it a try, here are a couple of options:

The 7 Minute Workout

Based on a 2013 article in the American College of Sports Medicine's *Health & Fitness Journal* and popularized by the *New York Times,* the 7 Minute Workout combines twelve simple, fast, scientifically proven exercises into a routine that lasts only, yep, seven minutes (thirty-second bursts with ten seconds of rest in between). You don't even have to think while you do it—there are apps to guide you through the moves; see maketimebook.com for recommendations.

JUMPING JACKS → WALL SIT → PUSH-UPS → ABDOMINAL CRUNCHES

CHAIR STEP-UPS → SQUATS → CHAIR TRICEPS DIPS → PLANK

HIGH KNEES RUNNING IN PLACE → LUNGES → PUSH-UPS WITH ROTATION → SIDE PLANK

JZ's 3×3 Workout

Or you could be like JZ and go even simpler. Three times a week, complete the following three steps:

1. As many push-ups as possible in one set, then rest one minute
2. As many squats as possible in one set, then rest one minute
3. As many lifts (pull-ups, curls, whatever) as possible in one set, then rest one minute

As many PUSH-UPS as possible → As many SQUATS as possible → As many LIFTS as possible

JZ

If I don't have time to go to the park to use the pull-up bar, I literally just lift things around the house. Like a chair, or a bag of books, or this end table we have that's cut out of a tree stump. It's not sophisticated, but it keeps my workouts short and simple. Plus, the act of lifting *stuff* (instead of weights or the handle of a gym machine) is closer to how our ancestors used their muscles in the real world: for lifting, carrying, and pushing.

To keep from getting bored—or if the exercises are too hard at first—experiment with variations. For example, do incline push-ups if regular ones are too hard. Or work your way up to one-legged squats if the standard version gets too easy. Just search online for "push-up variations," "squat variations," or "pull-up variations" to get ideas.

Eat Real Food

65. Eat Like a Hunter-Gatherer

This tactic is an unabashed homage to and rip-off of our hero Michael Pollan, a food enthusiast and author. In his bestselling book *In Defense of Food*, Pollan addressed the "supposedly incredibly complicated and confusing question of what we humans should eat in order to be maximally healthy":

Eat food. Not too much. Mostly plants.

Well, we read Pollan's books and tried his advice, and darned if it didn't work. Eating real food—in other words, nonprocessed ingredients Urk would recognize, such as plants, nuts, fish, and meat—made a huge difference in our energy levels. After all, the human body evolved to eat real food, so it's not surprising that your engine performs better when you give it the expected fuel.

JZ

In the early days of Make Time, I wanted to make time for cooking dinner at home. I considered it a double win: an energy-giving inconvenience (#63) and a way to make real food a staple of my everyday diet. I found that cooking with simple whole-food ingredients—like roasted meat with a salad—was much easier than following a long recipe point by point. For me, it was the best way to make a routine of eating like a hunter-gatherer.

Jake

To reset my default to eating more like a hunter-gatherer, I had to acknowledge that I need quick, easy snacks around at all times and then plan ahead to be sure those snacks are not only tasty but *also* real food. I buy almonds, walnuts, fruit, and peanut butter in bulk. Then, when I get hungry later, I'm ready with high-quality snacks I love: a handful of nuts and raisins or peanut butter on a banana or sliced apple. (See #68 for more snack talk.)

66. Central Park Your Plate

One simple technique to keep meals light and energizing is to **put salad on your plate first,** then add everything else around it. It's just like Central Park in New York City: You're reserving a big piece of territory for greens before you develop around the perimeter. More salad means less heavy food and, most likely, greater energy after eating.

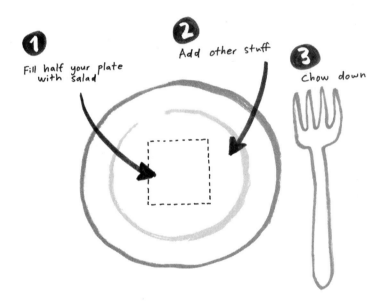

Tactic Battle: Fasting vs. Snacking

For JZ, fasting sharpens focus and improves energy. For Jake, the idea of going from lunch to dinner without a snack provokes anxiety.

67. Stay Hungry

JZ

The modern default is to eat constantly: three meals a day plus snacks to keep you from getting too hungry. But remember, Urk was a hunter-gatherer. He didn't eat unless he collected, caught, or killed his food. Can you imagine going out to gather berries or hunt for buffalo every morning, noon, and evening, plus any time in between when your blood sugar started to feel low?

The point is that just because we *can* eat all the time,

that doesn't mean we *should*. Even though we're lucky enough to live in a world of abundant food, our bodies are still the same as Urk's, evolved to survive and thrive in a world where food was scarce.

Intermittent fasting has become a bit of a fad, but there are lots of reasons to try it beyond the endorsements of Beyoncé and Benedict Cumberbatch. Food tastes better when you're hungry, and there are some great health benefits from fasting: cardiovascular fitness, longevity, muscle development, and maybe even reduced cancer risk.

But when it comes to energizing and making time, one benefit tops them all: Fasting (to a point) makes your mind clear and your brain sharp, which is great for staying focused on your priorities.

I've been practicing intermittent fasting—which is just a fancy name for "not eating sometimes"—for a couple of years. At first, the hunger was distracting. But after a few attempts, I got used to how it felt to be hungry, and I found it allowed me to tap into a new reserve of mental energy.[5] It's especially useful as part of my morning routine, in which I wake up and work for four or five hours (distraction-free and often food-free as well) on my Highlight.

Don't worry, I'm not suggesting going days without eating; simply try skipping a meal or even a snack. Of course, no one wants to be the guy who shows up to a business lunch or a birthday dinner and orders a seltzer with lime. But my friend Kevin introduced me to a fasting method that fits nicely into normal life. He'll eat an early dinner, then

---

5   Jake compared me to a house cat that becomes more energetic and huntery just before mealtime. I'm not sure how I should feel about the comparison, although my pet cats have assured me it's a good thing.

skip breakfast and have a big lunch as his next meal. That works out to roughly a sixteen-hour fast, and you can do it occasionally without anyone thinking you're too strange.

68. Snack Like a Toddler

Jake

Toddlers get cranky when they're hungry.[6] As a parent, I've seen this many times. Oh, lord, so many times.

But it's not the toddlers' fault. It's tough for a three-year-old to make it all the way from lunch till dinner without a pick-me-up. In fact, it's tough for a lot of grown-ups. Truth be told, I myself often get hungry and cranky without realizing it. So—unlike JZ, who avoids snacking—I think regular snacks are a good thing. In fact, I'm a bit of a snack fanatic. I always carry a couple of Kind granola bars in my backpack in case of a snackmergency. I even modified our design sprint schedule to make time for snack breaks.

When it comes to snacking, I think two things are important: choosing high-quality snacks and snacking when your body and brain need it, not just for something to do.

---

6   If any toddlers are reading this, no offense, but you know it's true.

To keep your battery charged, pretend you're a toddler or, more accurately, the parent of a toddler. Look out for crankiness and frustration and be prepared with a nutritious remedy. When you leave home in the morning, pack a little trail mix or an apple. If you find yourself hungry and snackless, seek out real food (e.g., bananas or nuts) instead of junk food (candy or chips). You wouldn't give your three-year-old a pack of Twizzlers to tide him over until lunch, and you should treat yourself with the same care. Grown-ups are people, too.

69. Go on the Dark Chocolate Plan

Sugar causes sugar highs, and sugar highs cause sugar crashes. Most people know that avoiding sugary treats is a great way to keep your energy up, but let's face it, it can be pretty hard to stop eating desserts.

So don't stop. Instead, switch your default. Allow yourself to have dessert as long as it's dark chocolate.

Dark chocolate has way less sugar than most other treats, so you'll get less of a crash. Many studies[7] suggest that dark chocolate even has health benefits. And because it's rich and delicious, you won't have to eat as much to satisfy your craving. In short, dark chocolate is freaking awesome and you should have it more often.[8]

---

7   Financed by chocolate companies, but whatever.

8   Just remember—dark chocolate has caffeine in it, so include it in your caffeine calculus (see #75).

Jake

I have a serious sweet tooth, but I've been on the Dark Chocolate Plan since 2002. It all started on a road trip from Seattle to Portland with my wife, Holly. We stopped at a gas station, where I purchased and subsequently consumed a large Coke, a pack of Bottle Caps candy, and a Jolly Rancher lollipop. Riding the sugar high, I proceeded to perform a five-minute pantomime of the video game Super Mario Bros., complete with sound effects.

Then came the cataclysmic sugar crash. I spent the rest of the drive slumped in the passenger seat complaining about my pounding headache while Holly laughed.

The Jolly Rancher Incident (as it would come to be known) finally made the connection in my head: Eat lots of sugar, feel lousy afterward. This was around the time all those studies about the health benefits of dark chocolate were in the news, so I decided to try it in place of my normal dessert regimen. At first, I had to get used to the bitter taste. But once my palate adapted, regular desserts seemed much too sweet.

I still eat ice cream or a cookie at least twice a week, but those are intentional treats. By default, I eat dark chocolate, my energy level stays stable, and my wife doesn't make fun of me . . . at least not about the Jolly Rancher Incident.

Optimize Caffeine

It's easy to get stuck in a default caffeine habit—like pouring yourself a coffee each time you take a stretch break at work. Caffeine is a (mildly) addictive drug, so even small unintentional behaviors like drinking a cup just to have a reason to get up from your desk can quickly become chemically reinforced habits. Hey, no judgment here. We're caffeine users ourselves, as are most humans.[9] But caffeine is powerful stuff, and because it has a direct effect on your energy level, you should drink it with intention rather than on autopilot.

We started thinking more about caffeine after meeting Ryan Brown. Ryan is serious about coffee. So serious that he's traveled the world in search of the perfect beans, started his own coffee delivery company, worked for high-end coffee titans Stumptown and Blue Bottle, and even written a book about coffee.

Ryan is also serious about the way he *drinks* coffee. For years, he's scoured every article and every new academic study on caffeine, trying to optimize his energy level by figuring out the best time to drink each cup. As you can imagine, when he offered to share what he'd discovered, we were all ears.

Ryan says that for him, maximizing energy started with understanding a bit about how caffeine works. To the brain, caffeine molecules look a lot like a molecule called *adenosine*, whose job is to tell the brain to slow down and feel sleepy or groggy. Adenosine is helpful in the evening as you get ready for bed. But when adenosine makes us sleepy in the morning or afternoon, we usually reach for caffeine.

When caffeine shows up, the brain says, "Hey good-lookin'!" and the caffeine binds to the receptors where the adenosine is supposed to

---

9   According to the U.S. Food and Drug Administration, around the world, 90 percent of adults consume caffeine in one form or another. In the United States, 80 percent of adults drink it every day, and that includes both Jake and JZ.

go. The adenosine is left to just float around, and as a result, the brain doesn't get the sleepy signal.

What's interesting in this (at least to us) is that caffeine doesn't technically give you an energy boost; instead, it blocks you from having an energy dip caused by adenosine-induced sleepiness. But once the caffeine wears off, all that adenosine is still hanging around, ready to pounce. If you don't recaffeinate, you crash. And over time, your body adjusts to more and more caffeine by producing more and more adenosine to compensate. This is why, if you normally drink lots of caffeine, you probably feel extra groggy and headachy when you don't have it.

Knowing all this, Ryan devised a perfect system that allowed him to enjoy as much coffee as possible, maintain steady energy, and not fry his nerves or disrupt his sleep. In the end, his personalized formula, backed by science and proven by experience, was crazy simple:

- Wake up without caffeine (in other words, get out of bed, eat breakfast, and start the day without any coffee).
- Have the first cup between 9:30 and 10:30 a.m.
- Have the last cup between 1:30 and 2:30 p.m.

That's it. Most days, Ryan drinks only two or three cups of coffee. This is a guy who *wrote a book about coffee*—he loves the stuff. But he also knows that if he drinks more or drinks it earlier or later, he actually has *less* energy, so instead, he limits his intake and savors every sip.

If Ryan already did all the hard work, we can just follow the same schedule, right? Not so fast. He cautioned us that there is no one-size-fits-all formula. Every person processes and reacts to caffeine in a slightly different way, depending on metabolism, body size, tolerance, and even DNA.

Of course, we decided to experiment for ourselves. What worked for JZ didn't always work for Jake, and vice versa. We had to customize our own formulas, but it was worth the trouble—we both ended up with steadier energy throughout the day.

We recommend experimenting with the following tactics and, as with all the tactics in this book, taking notes (pages 241 and 271) to track your results. Expect a lag time of three to ten days with some grogginess as your body adjusts.

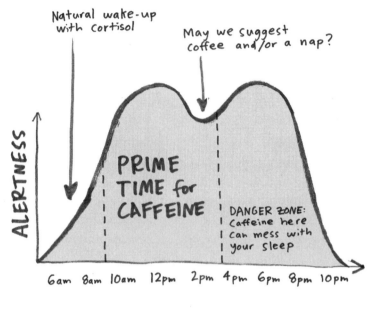

Natural wake-up with cortisol

May we suggest coffee and/or a nap?

ALERTNESS

PRIME TIME for CAFFEINE

DANGER ZONE: Caffeine here can mess with your sleep

6am 8am 10am 12pm 2pm 4pm 6pm 8pm 10pm

Source: We made this up (but it seems about right).

70. Wake Up *Before* You Caffeinate

In the morning, your body naturally produces lots of cortisol, a hormone that helps you wake up. When cortisol is high, caffeine doesn't do much for you (except for temporarily relieving your caffeine addiction symptoms). For most folks, cortisol is highest between 8 a.m. and 9 a.m., so for ideal morning energy, experiment with having that first cup of coffee at 9:30 a.m.

Jake

I made this switch after talking to Ryan. Before, I always woke up in a caffeine-withdrawal fog. It took me a few days to get over my morning grogginess, but once I did, I loved waking up alert. And now I feel like I get a bigger boost from my 9:30 a.m. coffee.

71. Caffeinate *Before* You Crash

The tricky thing about caffeine is that if you wait to drink it until you get tired, it's too late: The adenosine has already hooked up with your brain, and it's hard to shake the lethargy. We'll repeat that because it's a crucial detail: *If you wait until you get tired, it's too late.* Instead, think about when your energy regularly dips—for most of us, it's after lunch—and have coffee (or your caffeinated beverage of choice) thirty minutes beforehand. Or, as an alternative . . .

72. Take a Caffeine Nap

One slightly complicated but high-yield way to take advantage of caffeine mechanics is to wait till you get tired, drink some caffeine, then immediately take a fifteen-minute nap. The caffeine takes a while to be absorbed into your bloodstream and reach the brain. During your light sleep, the brain clears out the adenosine. When you wake up, the receptors are clear and the caffeine has just shown up. You're fresh, recharged, and ready to go. Studies have shown that caffeine naps improve cognitive and memory performance more than coffee or a nap alone does.[10]

JZ

I used caffeine naps for an afternoon boost while writing *Sprint*. For me, a good fifteen-minute caffeine nap gives me about two hours of focused energy.

73. Maintain Altitude with Green Tea

To keep a steady energy level throughout the day, try replacing high doses of caffeine (such as a giant cup of brewed coffee) with more frequent low doses. Green tea is a great option. The easiest and cheapest way to run this experiment is to buy a box of green tea bags and try substituting two or three cups of tea for every cup of coffee you'd normally have. This keeps your energy level more consistent and steady throughout the day, avoiding the energy peaks and valleys you get from something super caffeinated like coffee.

---

10 A 1997 study at Loughborough University tested participants with a driving simulator. People who took a caffeine nap outperformed people who only napped and people who only had caffeine. A 2003 study at Hiroshima University in Japan tried to help just-plain-nappers catch up with caffeine nappers by exposing them to bright lights, but the caffeine nappers still outperformed them on memory tests.

JZ

You also can try the Italian solution: the classic espresso. If you like espresso—which I do—and have access to it— which I *occasionally* do—it's another great low-dose option. A single espresso is roughly comparable to half a cup of coffee or two cups of green tea.

74. Turbo Your Highlight

Life is a lot like the video game Mario Kart: You've got to use your turbo boosts strategically. Try to time your caffeine intake so that you're wired right when you start your Highlight. Both of us apply this technique in the same simple way: We make a cup of coffee just before we sit down to write.

75. Learn Your Last Call

Jake's friend Camille Fleming is a doctor of family medicine who trains resident physicians at Swedish Hospital in Seattle. One of the most common complaints she hears from patients of all ages is difficulty sleeping. The first question she asks them—and the question she trains her students to ask—is "How much caffeine do you consume, and when?" Most people don't know the answer. Others say something like "Oh, that's not what's keeping me up; I have my last cup of coffee at 4 p.m."

What most people (including us before Camille explained it to Jake) don't realize is that the half-life of caffeine is five to six hours. So if the average person has a coffee at 4 p.m., half the caffeine is out of the bloodstream by 9 or 10 p.m., but the other half is still around. The upshot is that at least *some* caffeine is blocking at least *some* adenosine receptors for many hours after you have caffeine and very possibly interfering with your sleep and in turn the next day's energy.

You've got to experiment to figure out your own unique "Last Call for Caffeine," but if you have trouble sleeping, your last call might be earlier than you think. Experiment with cutting yourself off earlier and earlier and note if and when it becomes easier to fall asleep.

76. Disconnect Sugar

It's no secret that many caffeinated drinks are also very sugary: soft drinks such as Coke and Pepsi and sweetened drinks like Snapple teas and Starbucks mochas, not to mention turbocharged energy drinks such as Red Bull, Macho Buzz, and Psycho Juice.[11] But although sugar provides an immediate rush, you don't need us to tell you that it isn't good for sustained energy.

We're realists, and we won't tell you to cut sugar out of your diet entirely (we sure haven't). But we do suggest you consider separating the caffeine from the sweets.

---

11 We're pretty sure at least one of those is a real thing.

Jake

For me, caffeine used to mean a Coke or, if I was feeling fancy, a mocha. Switching wasn't easy, so I transitioned gradually, using unsweetened iced tea and iced coffee with cream as my gateways back from the land of syrup. Now, if I really want a sugary treat with my caffeine, I just have it separately. A coffee and a cookie is a lot more enjoyable than a coffee with a cookie dissolved in it, which is basically what soda is.

Go Off the Grid

77. Get Woodsy

78. Trick Yourself into Meditating

79. Leave Your Headphones at Home

80. Take Real Breaks

77. Get Woodsy

The woods sure are nice.

—JAKE'S DAD

Since 1982, the Japanese government has been encouraging a practice called *shinrin-yoku*, which can be translated as "forest bathing" or, more simply, "taking in the forest atmosphere." Studies on *shinrin-yoku* show that even brief exposure to a forest lowers stress, heart rate, and blood pressure. And it's not just in Japan; a 2008 University of Michigan study compared the cognitive performance of people who had just taken a walk in the city with that of people who had just taken a walk in a park. The nature walkers did 20 percent better.

So a little exposure to nature can make you measurably calmer and sharper. How does this work? The best explanation we could find comes from Cal Newport in *Deep Work:*

> *When walking through nature, you're freed from having to direct your attention, as there are few challenges to navigate (like crowded street crossings), and experience enough interesting stimuli to keep your mind sufficiently occupied to avoid the need to actively aim your attention. This state allows your directed attention resources time to replenish.*

In other words, the forest recharges the battery in your brain. Maybe it strikes a chord with our Urk ancestry. Whatever the explanation, it's worth a try, and you don't have to hike the Pacific Crest Trail. Heck, you don't even need a forest; the benefits seem to start with any natural surroundings. Just experiment with spending a few minutes in a park and take note of what it does for your mental energy. If you can't get to the park, step outside for a breath of fresh air. Even if you just crack a window, we predict you'll feel better. Our hunter-gatherer bodies feel more alive outdoors.

Jake

My dad loved the woods, but he worked as a lawyer, and his weekdays usually were spent in offices and his car. So whenever he had a break between meetings, he'd head to a nearby park and walk the trails. Every Saturday and every Sunday, he took a walk in the woods. The weather didn't matter. Unless the wind was so strong that he thought a tree might fall on him, he always made time for nature.

As a kid, I thought Dad's forest obsession was a little wacky. But as a grown-up, I get it. When I started my career and my brain was inundated by the endless noise and busyness of the work world, I realized something magical happened when I took a walk in the park. It was like my brain settled down and my thoughts became clearer—not just during the walk but for many hours afterward. Nowadays, a run through the woods of Golden Gate Park is one of my daily habits. When I get off the city streets and hit the trail, my head seems to loosen up and my stress evaporates. I guess Dad was right—the woods sure are nice.

78. Trick Yourself into Meditating

The benefits of meditation are well documented. It reduces stress. It increases happiness. It recharges your brain and boosts focus. But there are problems. Meditation is difficult, and you might feel a little silly doing it. We get it. We still feel embarrassed when we talk about meditation. In fact, we are embarrassed *right now* as we type these words.

But meditation is nothing to be ashamed of. **Meditation is just a breather for your brain.**

For human beings, thinking is the default position. Most of the time this is a good thing. But *constant* thinking means your brain never gets rest. When you meditate, instead of passively going along with the thoughts, you stay quiet and *notice* the thoughts, and that slows them down and gives your brain a break.

So okay, meditation is rest for your brain. But here's the crazy thing: **Meditation is also *exercise* for your brain.** Staying quiet and noticing your thoughts is refreshing, but ironically, it's also hard work. The act of slowing down and noticing your thoughts is exertion that leaves you invigorated, just as exercise does.

In fact, the effects of meditation look a lot like the effects of exercise. Studies show that meditation increases working memory and the ability to maintain focus.[12] Meditation even makes parts of the brain thicker and stronger, just as exercise builds muscle.[13]

But meditation is, as we said, hard work. And it can be hard to

---

12 For example, a 2013 study at the University of California, Santa Barbara found that students who meditated as little as ten minutes a day for two weeks improved their average GRE (Graduate Record Examinations, a super hard test) verbal scores from 460 to 520. That's a pretty awesome brain boost for a pretty minimal effort.

13 In 2006, researchers at Harvard, Yale, and MIT collaborated, using MRI scans to compare the brains of experienced meditators with those of non-meditators, and found that the meditators had thicker cortexes in areas associated with attention and sensory perception.

stay motivated when the results, unlike with exercise, aren't outwardly visible: Your cortex might bulk up, but you can't meditate your way to six-pack abs.

We also recognize that finding the time to stop everything you're doing to sit and notice your thoughts is quite difficult when you've got a million things to do. But the energy, focus, and mental calm you get out of it can actually *help you make time* to get those things done. So here's our meditation advice:

1. We're not even gonna try to tell you *how* you should meditate. We're not experts—but your smartphone is. To get started, use a guided meditation app. (See Jake's story on the next page and find our app recommendations on maketimebook.com.)

2. Aim low. Even a three-minute session can increase your energy. Ten minutes is awesome.

3. You don't have to sit in the lotus position. Try guided meditation while riding the bus, lying down, walking, running, or even eating.

4. If the word *meditation* feels uncomfortable to you, just call it something else. Try "quiet time," "resting," "pausing," "taking a break," or "doing a Headspace" (or whatever app you use).

5. Some people say meditation counts only if you do it unassisted for long periods. Those people are jerks. If it works for you and you're happy, you can keep doing short sessions of guided meditation forever.

Jake

For years, I heard great things about meditation, but I couldn't get into it. Then my wife persuaded me to try the Headspace app on my iPhone. "You'll like it," she said. "Andy is very plainspoken."

Andy is Andy Puddicombe, cofounder of Headspace and the voice in your headphones. His British accent took some getting used to, but Holly was right. I liked it a lot.

I started tracking how I felt after each session to see if Headspace improved my focus. It did.

WAS HEADSPACE WORTH IT?
- 4/19   10 min   YES
- 4/20   10 min   YES (easier to focus, calmer)
- 4/21   10 min   YES (moved slower & smarter when I started to work after)

Then I got way into a feature of the app that tracks how many days in a row you've meditated. Eventually, by squeezing in short sessions while riding the bus, I got my streak up to 400 days!

As I used Headspace, it became easier to concentrate for long periods. My thoughts had more clarity. And, though I know this sounds odd, I felt more willing to be myself. (Which I *think* is a good thing.)

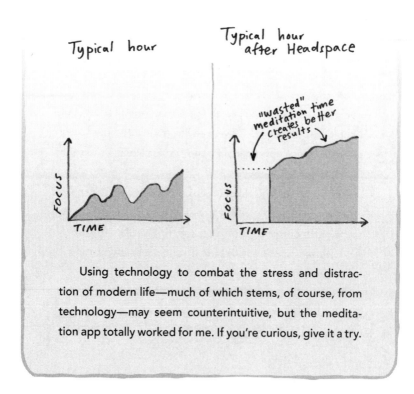

Typical hour

Typical hour after Headspace

"wasted" time meditation creates better results

FOCUS

TIME

FOCUS

TIME

Using technology to combat the stress and distraction of modern life—much of which stems, of course, from technology—may seem counterintuitive, but the meditation app totally worked for me. If you're curious, give it a try.

79. Leave Your Headphones at Home

Headphones are awesome. They're easy to take for granted, but the power they give us to listen to anything, anywhere, in complete privacy is nothing short of amazing. You can take Malcolm Gladwell on a jog, crank up Joan Jett while you work, or listen to a Dungeons & Dragons podcast while you sit on a crowded airplane. Nobody has to know what you're listening to. It's your own little universe, in stereo.

So, of course, a lot of modern life is spent wearing headphones to fill space in the day that otherwise might be quiet. But if you put on headphones every time you work, walk, exercise, or commute, your brain never gets any quiet. Even an album you've listened to a million times still creates a bit of mental work. Your music, podcast, or audiobook prevents boredom, but boredom creates space for thinking and focus (#57).

Take a break and leave your headphones at home. Just listen to the sounds of traffic, or the clack of your keyboard, or your footsteps on the pavement. Resist the itch to fill the blank space.

We're not saying you should give up on headphones altogether. That would be pretty hypocritical, because we use them ourselves almost every day. But an occasional headphone vacation for a day or just an hour is an easy way to put some quiet in your day and give your brain a moment to recharge.

80. Take Real Breaks

It's awfully tempting to check Twitter, Facebook, or another Infinity Pool app as a break from work. But these kinds of breaks don't renew or relax your brain. For one thing, when you see a troubling news story or an envy-inducing photo from a friend, you feel more stressed, not less. And if you work at a desk, Infinity Pool breaks keep you glued to your chair and away from energy-giving activities like moving around and talking to other people.

Instead, try to take breaks without screens: Gaze out the window (it's good for your eyes), go for a walk (it's good for your mind and body), grab a snack (it's good for your energy if you're hungry), or talk to someone (it's usually good for your mood unless you talk to a jerk).

If your default break is to check an Infinity Pool, you'll have to change your habits—and changing habits, as we've noted, is hard. We've found that these "speed bump" tactics you've already read about can help: Keep a distraction-free phone (#17), log out of addictive websites (#18), and put your toys away when you're done (#26). But once you start taking breaks in the real world, we think you'll love them. With more energy, it's easier to get back into Laser mode and sustain focus on your Highlight.

JZ

Even when I use the Make Time tactics, I still hear the siren song of Infinity Pools. After a good hour or even fifteen minutes of productive time, I'll often think to myself: "Man, that was a solid chunk of work. I should reward myself by checking Twitter!"

But it's amazing how the smallest speed bump can thwart that impulse and remind me to take a real break. For example, when I try to visit twitter.com on my computer and see a log-in screen, I remember: "Ah, yes, I should take a real break." This has become my new routine and my new default.

Jake

I love taking real-world breaks, but sometimes they're not enough. When I've been working super hard and I get that "brain drain" feeling like my head is a squeezed-out sponge, I know it's time to take a megabreak: I'll stop everything and watch a whole movie. Why a movie? Unlike a a TV series, a movie is relatively short and finite. Unlike social media or email or the news, it won't make me anxious. It's pure escapism and a chance for my brain to stop and relax without the risk of falling into a time crater of energy-draining distraction.

Make It Personal

81. Spend Time with Your Tribe
82. Eat Without Screens

81. Spend Time with Your Tribe

All of us, even the most introverted, have a hardwired need for human connection. This shouldn't come as a big surprise; after all, Urk lived among a tribe of 100 to 200 people. Humans evolved to thrive in tight-knit communities.

But today face-to-face time can be hard to come by. If you live in a city, you probably saw more humans yesterday than Urk saw in his entire life, but how many of them did you talk to? And how many of those conversations were meaningful? It's a cruel irony of modern life that we're surrounded by people yet more isolated than ever. This is a big deal, especially if you consider the findings from Harvard's 75-year Study of Adult Development: People with strong relationships are more likely to live long, healthy, fulfilling lives. We're not claiming that talking to strangers in the grocery store checkout line will help you live to be 100—but spending time with people face-to-face can be a big energy booster.

Even in the twenty-first century, you have a tribe. If you work in an office, you have colleagues. In your family, you might have siblings, parents, kids, and/or a significant other. And you (we hope) have friends. Sure, those people might annoy you or frustrate you sometimes, but more often than not, spending time with them is energizing.

When we say "spending time," we mean having real conversations with your voice, not just commenting on posts, clicking hearts and thumbs-ups, or sending emails, texts, photos, emojis, and animated GIFs. Screen-based communication is efficient, but that's part of the problem: It's so easy that it often displaces higher-value real-life conversations.

Not every person lifts our spirits, of course, but we all know a *few* people who give us energy *most* times we talk to them. Here's a simple experiment to try:

1. Think of one of those energy-giving people.
2. Go out of your way to have a real conversation with her or him. You can talk in person or on the phone, but your voice must be involved.
3. Afterward, note your energy level.

This conversation might be a meal with your family or a phone call to your brother. It can be with an old friend or someone you just met. The time and place don't really matter as long as you use your voice. Even if it's only once a week, reach out to friends whom you admire, who inspire you, who make you laugh, who let you be yourself. Spending time with interesting, high-energy people is one of the best—and most enjoyable—ways to recharge your battery.

Jake

I keep a list of "energy givers" in my phone's notes app: people who put a bounce in my step every time I see them. Yes, this is bizarre (and maybe a little creepy), but it helps me remember that taking the extra time to have coffee or lunch with one of these friends actually gives me *more* time in the day because I'm so energized afterward.

82. Eat Without Screens

When you eat without screens, you hit three of our five Energize principles at once. You're less likely to mindlessly shovel unhealthy food in your mouth, you're more likely to have an energizing face-to-face conversation with another human, and you're creating space in your day to give your brain a rest from its constant busyness. And all this while doing something you have to do anyway!

Jake

When I was growing up, my family ate dinner while watching television. So I was surprised when I met my then-girlfriend/future-wife's family, who ate dinner at a *dining table*. It seemed so antiquated. Would she expect me to do the same? But in those days, Holly and I didn't have a TV anyway, so when we moved in together, we adopted her family's style of screen-free dinners purely by default.

But the habit stuck even after we did get a television. By the time we had kids, I'd practically forgotten how I used to eat at the TV. And now, every evening, our family of four sits down to eat together. No TV, no phones, no iPads. Sure, this habit has cost me some familiarity with pop culture, but I wouldn't trade the extra hours it's given me with my wife and sons for anything.

Sleep in a Cave

83. Make Your Bedroom a Bed Room

For Urk, bedtime would have marked the end of an hours-long process to remove mental stimuli gradually and shift into sleep. When you look at social media, email, or the news before bed, you sabotage this process. Instead of winding down, you're revving your brain up. An annoying email or distressing news story can make your mind race and keep you awake for hours.

If you want to improve your sleep, keep the phone out of your bedroom—at all times. And don't stop there. Remove *all* electronic devices to transform your bedroom into a true sanctuary for sleep. No TVs, no iPads. No Kindles with backlights. In other words: Make your bedroom a bed room.

Television presents its own challenges. A TV in your bedroom offers a very tempting path of least resistance. You don't have to do anything to be entertained—it does all the work! Television is particularly dangerous because of the time involved. You lose sleep while you're watching, and you keep losing sleep after you shut it off and wait for your stimulated brain to transition into sleep mode.

Reading in bed is a wonderful alternative, but paper books or magazines are best. A Kindle is okay, too, because it's not loaded with apps and other distractions; just make sure to turn off the bright white backlight.

It can be tough to keep devices out of the bedroom, but it's easier to change your environment than to rely on willpower to change your behavior. Do it once and make it permanent: Physically remove the TV. Unplug your smartphone charger and get its stand or base out of your bedroom.

There's probably one device you'll need to keep in your bedroom: an alarm clock. Choose a simple model with a screen that's not too bright (or without a screen if you don't mind the ticking). If possible, put your alarm clock on a dresser or shelf across the room. This will keep the light away from your eyes, and it'll help you wake up: When the alarm sounds, you'll have no choice but to get out of bed, stretch your legs, and switch it off. We think that's a better way to start your day than snuggling with your smartphone.

84. Fake the Sunset

When we see bright light, our brains think, "It's morning. Time to wake up!" This is an ancient and automatic system. For Urk, the system worked great: He fell asleep when it got dark and woke when the sun rose. The natural cycle of the day helped regulate his sleep and energy.

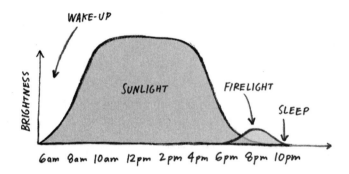

URK'S DAYS

But for modern humans, this poses a problem. Between our screens and our lightbulbs, we're simulating daylight right up until we climb into bed. It's as though we're telling our brains, "It's day, it's day, it's day, it's day—WHOA, IT'S NIGHT, GO TO BED." No wonder we have trouble sleeping.

MODERN DAYS

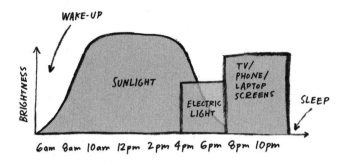

We're not the first to point out this problem. For years, people have been saying you should avoid looking at your phone or laptop in bed. That's good advice, but it's not enough. When JZ was trying to become a morning person, he discovered that he needed a bigger strategy. He needed to fake the sunset.

Here's how to do it:

1. Starting when you eat dinner or a few hours before your ideal bedtime, turn down the lights in your home. Switch off bright overhead lights. Instead, use dim table or side lamps. For bonus points, light candles at the dinner table.

2. Turn on your phone, computer, or TV's "night mode." These features shift screen colors from blue to red and orange. Instead of looking at a bright sky, it's like sitting around a campfire.

3. When you go to bed, kick all devices out of the room (see #83).

4. If sunlight or streetlight is still sneaking into your bedroom, try a simple sleep mask over your eyes. Yes, you will feel and look a little silly, but they work.

If you often feel lethargic or low-energy in the morning, try faking the sunrise, too. In recent years, automatic "dawn simulator" lights have become smaller and cheaper thanks to improved LED technology and a healthy market of people who hate winter mornings. The idea is simple: Before the alarm sounds, a bright light gradually turns on, simulating a perfectly timed sunrise and tricking your brain into waking up. If you combine that with turning down the lights in the evening, it's the next best thing to living in a cave.

85. Sneak a Nap

Napping makes you smarter. Seriously. Lots of studies[14] show that napping improves alertness and cognitive performance in the afternoon. As usual, we've tested the science ourselves.

Jake
I love naps, and not just because my name is Knapp.

---

14 There really are a lot, but by far the most influential was a 1994 study by NASA conducted on long-haul commercial pilots. The researchers found that pilots who took a nap improved their performance by 34 percent. The study was particularly influential because (a) we all want our pilots to perform well and (b) we can all agree that NASA is totally badass.

You don't even have to fall asleep. Just lying down and resting for ten to twenty minutes can be a great way to recharge.

But the truth is that it's really hard to take a nap if you work in an office. Even at offices with fancy nap pods (we've worked in them), most people don't feel like they have time to nap, and let's face it, pod or no pod, it can still feel very awkward to sleep at work. If you can't sleep on the job, consider napping at home. Even if you only nap on the weekend, you'll benefit.

86. Don't Jet-Lag Yourself

Sometimes, despite our best efforts, we fall behind on sleep. We have a busy week, an ill-timed flight, or some stress or worry that keeps us up at night, and we find ourselves with that all too familiar feeling of being overtired.

We were talking about sleep challenges with our friend Kristen Brillantes, who's one of the most ambitious and productive people we know. (You may remember Kristen and her Sour Patch Kid method for saying no from tactic #12.) In addition to her day job as a design producer at Google, she's a food-truck owner and a life coach for all kinds of entrepreneurs and young professionals.

"It's tempting to try catching up by sleeping late," Kristen said. "The problem is, it doesn't work."

She told us that sleeping late on weekends is basically like giving yourself jet lag: It confuses your internal clock and makes it even harder to bounce back from the original deficit. So just as you would when traveling to a different time zone, she recommends resisting the temptation to oversleep and trying to stick as closely as possible to your regular schedule.

"Sleep debt" is a real thing, and it's bad news for your health, wellness, and ability to focus. But one Saturday of sleeping until noon— glorious as that is—won't do much to pay off your debt. Instead, you need to chip away at it, using the tactics in this chapter to help you catch up by sleeping well in day-by-day installments. So to keep your battery charged, keep that alarm set to the same time every day whether it's a weekday, weekend, or holiday.

We have one more note about building energy. If you're in a time of life when your primary responsibility is taking care of someone else— whether it's a young child, a spouse, a friend, or a parent—many of these tactics might seem a bit self-indulgent, if not totally impractical. If so, we'd like to suggest a special tactic, one designed to give you permission to take care of yourself.

87. Put On Your Own Oxygen Mask First

When Jake's wife was pregnant with their first child, they took a class for new parents. The teacher offered a great piece of advice: Put on your own oxygen mask first.

On airplanes, they tell you to put on your own mask before assisting other passengers. The rationale is that if the cabin pressure drops (let's not think about *that* too much), everybody will need oxygen. But if you pass out while trying to help someone . . . well, that isn't very helpful, is it? It may be heroic, but it's not wise.

A newborn baby is kind of like a loss of cabin pressure, and if you don't take care of yourself (at least a little), you can't be a great caretaker. That means you need to maximize your energy by eating as well as you can and making the most of whatever sleep you can get. You've got to find a way to take little breaks and maintain your sanity. In other words, you should put on your own oxygen mask first.

Even if you're caring for someone other than a newborn, this advice is important to keep in mind. The everyday needs of another person, especially someone you love, can consume a tremendous amount of emotional and physical energy. Again, we know the idea of trying some of these tactics—going for a walk, taking quiet time alone, or getting in a workout—might seem selfish. But remember, the tactics in this section are all meant to give you the energy to make time for the things that matter. If you're caring for a loved one, what could matter more?

ENERGIZE

Reflect

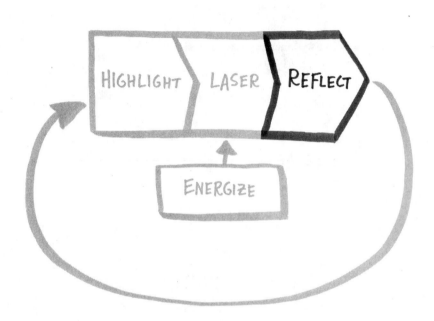

Science and everyday life cannot
and should not be separated.

—ROSALIND FRANKLIN

Welcome to the fourth and final step of Make Time. In "Reflect,"
you'll use a little science to tailor the system to you: your habits, your
lifestyle, your preferences, and even your unique body.

Fine-Tune Your Days with the Scientific Method

Don't worry, science is simple. Sure, some of it—particle accelerators,
astrophysics, photon torpedoes—can be a little tricky. But the scientific method itself is straightforward:

1. **OBSERVE** what's going on.
2. **GUESS** why things are happening the way they are.
3. **EXPERIMENT** to test your hypothesis.
4. **MEASURE** the results and decide whether you were right.

That's pretty much it. The scientific know-how behind everything from WD-40 to the Hubble space telescope all came from following those four steps.

Make Time uses the scientific method, too. Everything in this book is based on our observations about the modern world and our guesses about why bad things happen to our time and attention. You might boil Make Time down to three hypotheses:

The Highlight hypothesis
If you set a single intention at the start of each day, we predict you'll be more satisfied, joyful, and effective.

The Laser hypothesis
If you create barriers around the Busy Bandwagon and the Infinity Pools, we predict you'll focus your attention like a laser beam.

The Energize hypothesis
If you live a little more like a prehistoric human, we predict you'll enhance your mental and physical energy.

The tactics in this book are eighty-seven experiments for testing these hypotheses. We've tried them on ourselves. But only you can test them on *you*. And for that, you need the scientific method. You need to measure the data—not in a double-blind study of unwitting university students or in some sterile laboratory—but in your own everyday life.

You are a sample size of one, and your results are the only results that really matter. This kind of everyday science is what "Reflect" is all about.

Take Notes to Track Your Results (and Keep You Honest)

Collecting the data is super easy. Every day you'll reflect on whether you made time for your Highlight and how well you were able to focus on it. You'll note how much energy you had. You'll review the tactics you used, jot down some observations on what worked and what didn't, and make a plan for which tactics you'll try tomorrow.

This step takes only a few moments; you just answer these simple questions:

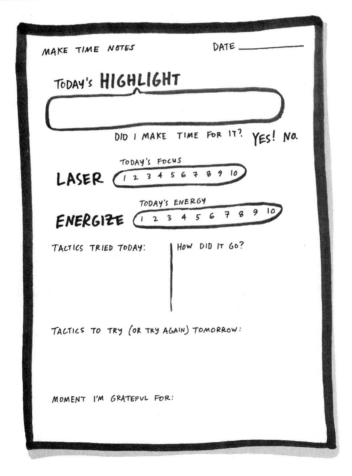

Here's an example of what yours might look like on a typical day.

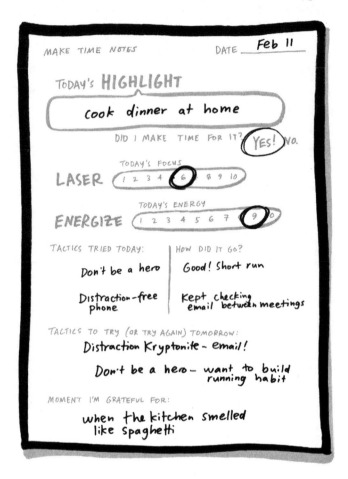

MAKE TIME NOTES   DATE **Feb 11**

TODAY'S **HIGHLIGHT**

cook dinner at home

DID I MAKE TIME FOR IT? **YES!** No.

TODAY'S FOCUS

LASER   1 2 3 4 **6** 7 8 9 10

TODAY'S ENERGY

ENERGIZE   1 2 3 4 5 6 7 **9** 10

TACTICS TRIED TODAY:	HOW DID IT GO?
Don't be a hero	Good! Short run
Distraction-free phone	Kept checking email between meetings

TACTICS TO TRY (OR TRY AGAIN) TOMORROW:

Distraction Kryptonite - email!

Don't be a hero - want to build running habit

MOMENT I'M GRATEFUL FOR:

when the kitchen smelled like spaghetti

This page is designed to help you keep track of how you use Make Time, of course. But it's also designed to help you learn about *you*. After a few days of taking notes, you'll find yourself more aware of your energy and attention throughout the day and more in control of where you direct it.

As you experiment with the system, it's important to remember that some tactics will work right away but some will require patience and perseverance. Sometimes it takes trial-and-error to make a tactic fit in your life (*Should I run or ride a stationary bike? Before work, at lunch, or in the evening?*). If you fail at first, don't be hard on yourself. Give it time and use the notes to track and tweak your approach. Remember that perfection is not the goal. This isn't about building up to doing all the tactics all the time or even doing some of the tactics all the time. You'll have off days and off weeks, and that's fine. You can restart your experiments at any time, and you can do as much or as little as fits in your life.

The main purpose of these notes is to measure the results of your experiments, but you'll notice that we included a question about gratitude. Gratitude rituals have been showing up in different cultures for thousands of years: They're central to Buddhism and Stoicism; they're in the Bible; they're part of Japanese tea ceremonies; and, of course, they're the foundation (and namesake) of our Thanksgiving holiday. But regardless of its illustrious history, we're including gratitude for a very simple reason: We want to bias the results of your experiments.

Changing defaults isn't always easy, so it's helpful to look back on the day through a grateful lens. Quite often you'll find that even if lots of things didn't go your way, your hard work of making time still paid off with a moment you're grateful for. When that happens, the feeling of gratitude becomes a powerful incentive to do the steps again tomorrow.

You'll find an empty notes page at the end of the book (page 271). Photocopy it or go to maketimebook.com for a printable PDF and a variety of paper and digital formats. Of course, you can just answer these questions on plain paper or in a regular notebook.

We also recommend setting recurring reminders on your phone to help reinforce your new Make Time habits. This is as simple as saying "Hey Siri,[1] every morning at 9 a.m., remind me to choose a Highlight" and "Every evening at 9 p.m., remind me to take notes on my day."

Reflecting on your day may become a permanent habit, but even if

---

1   Or "Okay, Google" or "Hello, HAL" or whatever.

you just do it for the first couple of weeks, that's fine. The Make Time notes shouldn't feel like (yet another) obligation in your life; it's just a way to learn about yourself and fine-tune the system to work best for you.

Small Shifts Create Big Results

At the beginning of this book, we made some crazy assertions. We said it was possible to slow down the rush of modern life, feel less busy, and enjoy your days more. Now that we've gone through all four steps, it's time to take another look at those claims. Can you *really* make time every day?

We admit we don't have a magic reset button for your life. If you have to answer five hundred emails today, you probably can't get away with answering zero tomorrow. If your schedule was packed this week, it'll probably be packed next week, too. We can't erase your calendar or freeze your inbox.

But such radical changes aren't necessary. There's an invisible premise behind Make Time: You're *already* close. Small shifts can put you in control. If you reduce a few distractions, increase your physical and mental energy just a bit, and focus your attention on one bright spot, a blah day can become extraordinary. It doesn't require an empty calendar—just sixty to ninety minutes of attention on something special. The goal is to make time for what matters, find more balance, and enjoy today a little more.

Jake

Back in 2008, I started taking daily notes to help me record my energy level and try to figure out how to improve it. Here's an excerpt:

Nov. 17
Energy level: 8

Tactics tried today:
Exercised this morning for 30 minutes.

How did it go?
Seemed to feel extra good afterward. I should try that more in the future. I focused for three straight hours in the morning but then felt tired after lunch. There was a really good dessert, though, and I had two (chocolate cake). Maybe I should not have dessert after lunch.

These notes are packed with insights: Exercise in the morning gave me a boost,[2] dessert at lunch made me feel lousy in the afternoon, and three hours might be my outer limit for focused work.

Sure, the insights ("Exercise is good, sugar is bad") aren't groundbreaking. But even if they should have been obvious, recording them for myself was powerful. It's one

---

2   This was not long after my "don't be a hero" realization about exercise (see #61).

thing to read about a research study in the news and quite another to experience the results firsthand.

The daily notes helped me find pitfalls to avoid as well as bright spots to reproduce. I started finding ways to move my body in the morning, and after a couple of months, my morning exercise routine began to stick. I adjusted my schedule to eat lunch earlier, before I was ravenous, which helped me switch my default to lighter and more energizing lunches.

My early notes were all about Energize, but later I saw how useful it could be to track my Highlight and Laser tactics as well. These one-person experiments helped me figure out my tactics and adjust my personal version of the system. And the daily reflection changed my behavior for the better: I'm always more diligent when somebody's watching, even when that somebody is me.

Start "Someday" Today

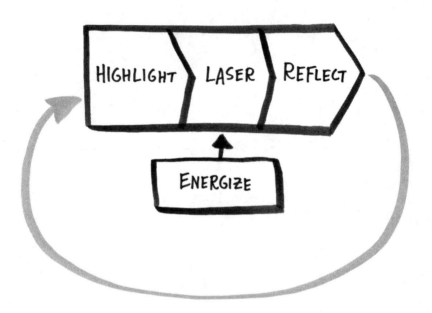

Do not ask yourself what the world needs.
Ask yourself what makes you come alive,
and then go do that. Because what the world
needs is people who have come alive.

—HOWARD THURMAN

We each spent years in Silicon Valley, where one of the favorite business terms is *pivot*. In startup-speak, a pivot is when a company starts out doing one thing but realizes that a related (or sometimes unrelated) idea is more promising. If they have enough confidence (and funding), they'll pivot to the new direction.

Some of these startup pivots have been fantastically successful. A shopping tool called Tote pivoted and became Pinterest. A podcasting company called Odeo pivoted and became Twitter. An app called Burbn for checking in to restaurants and bars pivoted and became Instagram, and a company making an operating system for cameras pivoted and became Android.

Once you become confident with the tools and tactics of Make Time, you may find yourself ready to make a pivot of your own. As you become more aware of your priorities through choosing Highlights and increasing your focus through Laser mode, you may find new strengths and interests emerging—and also build the confidence to follow them and see where they lead. That's exactly what happened to us.

Jake

I started my time experiments to become more productive at work, but the result was something much greater. The tactics in this book helped me find more balance at work and at home. By making my days a tiny bit different, I felt vastly more in control. As I learned how to make time for my own priorities, cool projects emerged, like developing the design sprint method, doing art shows with my kids, and, of course, writing. Starting and finishing my first book was tough, but Make Time helped me do it.

Eventually, a funny thing happened. The more I made time for writing, the more I wanted to write. Finally, I decided to try doing it as a full-time job. This major shift in my priorities didn't happen overnight. It was like a snowball rolling downhill, growing with every revolution. It took seven years from starting to make time for writing in the evenings back in 2010 to becoming a full-time writer in 2017. But when the time came, the decision to leave Google—which once would have seemed insane to me—was easy. What I wanted was clear, and I'd built the confidence to know I could give it a shot.

JZ

Like Jake, I began using the tactics in this book to be more efficient at work, but as time went by, I realized I didn't want to use my increased energy and focus to climb the corporate ladder. Instead, a new priority emerged: sailing. The more time I invested in sailing, the more satisfaction I got back. But unlike work, the satisfaction from sailing wasn't tied to external rewards; it was an intrinsic motivation that came from learning hands-on skills, seeing the world from a different perspective, and finding joy in the process.

I began looking for ways to make more time for sailing. And with the tactics in this book, that's exactly what I did. My wife, Michelle, and I began to explore the possibility of a life under sail: living aboard, traveling when we wanted, and making an even larger commitment to our outside-the-office passion. In 2017, we went for it. We quit our jobs, gave up our apartment, moved onto our sailboat, and began sailing the Pacific Coast from California south into Mexico and Central America.

As I embraced sailing, other priorities slipped away. By stepping away from corporate life to sail and travel full-time, I gave up my fancy job title, cool office, salary, and annual bonus. But for me, after years following the system you've just read about, making the trade-off was an easy choice. I knew what I wanted to make time for, so I did.

For much of our own careers, we were too distracted, scrambled, busy, and exhausted to make time for the things we cared most about. First, Make Time helped us find control. Over time, it helped us start those classic "someday" projects we had been putting off for years and could have continued putting off indefinitely.

When you create a practice of setting *your own* most important priority, daily life changes. Perhaps you'll find your inner compass perfectly aligned with your current work, in which case you'll now be that much more capable of identifying and acting on the most important opportunities. Make Time could provide a long-term sustained boost to your career. Your hobbies and side projects, strengthened with Make Time, could be a perfect complement.

But it is also possible that those side projects might gradually take on a life of their own. A new and unexpected path may emerge. And you may find yourself ready to follow that path and see where it goes.

Just to be clear, we aren't advising you to quit your job and sail around the world (unless that's what you're into, in which case you should email JZ for advice). And we should emphasize that we don't claim to have it all figured out—not hardly! We're constantly rebalancing our priorities, and it's extremely unlikely that what either of us is doing today is what he'll be doing two, five, or ten years from now. By the time you read this, we may have changed course yet again, and that's fine. As long as we're making time for what matters to us, the system is working.

Regardless of whether your goal is to find more balance in life, grow in your current career, or even pivot to a new one, we predict that Make Time will create more time and attention for the things you're passionate about. As Howard Thurman said, the world needs people who have come alive. Don't wait for "someday" to make time for what makes *you* come alive. Start today.

"QUICK START" GUIDE TO MAKE TIME

There are a lot of tactics in this book. If you're not sure where to begin, try this recipe:

Highlight: Schedule Your Highlight (#8)
A simple way to be proactive, give form to your day, and break the reaction cycle.

Laser: Block Distraction Kryptonite (#24)
Free yourself from one Infinity Pool, and see how your attention changes.

Energize: Pound the Pavement (#62)
A few minutes of walking each day provides a boost for the body and quiet for the mind.

Reflect every evening for three days
Don't worry about committing to a lifetime of evening journaling (we're not there yet, either). Just try the three tactics above and, for three days straight, take notes in the evening. See what you learn and take it from there.

Also, check out maketimebook.com for tips and apps to help you start.

SAMPLE AGENDAS

We thought it might be helpful to see what Make Time looks like in everyday life, so here are some typical days from our calendars. It's possible to fit a *lot* of tactics into one day, and that's not even counting tactics like Design Your Day, Log Out, Wear a Wristwatch, and Try a Distraction-Free Phone that don't show up on the calendar. But even though it's possible to fit a lot in, it isn't necessary. These are extreme cases—remember, we're Time Dorks.

Jake

When my schedule was packed with meetings, I'd use several tactics to build and maintain my energy throughout the day. By preserving energy, I was able to make time in the evening for writing my adventure novel.

6am		
7am	Wake up and eat breakfast	
8am	Walk Luke to school, run home through the park	← Get woodsy
9am	Bus to work, listen to Headspace	← Trick yourself into meditating
10am	Meeting	
11am	Meeting	
12pm	Lunch with a friend	← Eat without screens
1pm	Meeting	
2pm		
3pm	Meeting	← Snack like a toddler
4pm	Meeting	
5pm	Bus home, no headphones	
6pm	Dinner with family	←
7pm	Play with Flynn, then Flynn to bed	← Spend time with your tribe
8pm	Spend time with Holly and Luke	↙
9pm		
10pm	Work on adventure novel	← HIGHLIGHT!
11pm	Go to bed	

JZ

This is what a normal weekday looked like for me when I was working at Google. Every day, I would wake up early and *immediately* spend time on my Highlight before doing *anything* else—except drinking coffee, of course. My walk to work would start the day with an energy boost. Then, later in the day, as my creative energy waned, I shifted my focus to administrative work (such as email) and rebuilding my energy (by exercising, cooking, and spending time with my wife, Michelle).

6am	Wake up and make coffee	
7am	Working Block #1: Highlight time!	← HIGHLIGHT!
8am	Shower and get ready	
9am	Walk to work	↙ Pound the pavement
10am	Working Block #2: Other projects	← Block your calendar
11am		
12pm	Big lunch alone: Time to read	← Stay hungry (first food of the day)
1pm	Make espresso and drink it!	
2pm	Meeting	
3pm	Meeting	
4pm	Working Block #3: Email	← Email at the end of the day
5pm	Bus home: More time to read	
6pm	Grocery store	
7pm	3x3 workout	
8pm	Time with Michelle, making dinner	← Spend time with your tribe
9pm	One episode of TV	
10pm	Go to bed	
11pm		

FURTHER READING FOR TIME DORKS

The Happiness Project by Gretchen Rubin
This book will make you happier. You would be crazy not to read it.

Brain Rules by John Medina
A fun and fast overview of brain science, easy to understand and easy to remember. (For a much harder read with a lot more detail, check out *The Distracted Mind: Ancient Brains in a High-Tech World* by Adam Gazzaley and Larry Rosen.)

Deep Work by Cal Newport
Packed with opinionated and often unusual strategies for doing focused work.

The 4-Hour Workweek by Tim Ferriss
Tim is a superhuman and we're not, but we still learned a lot from this book.

Getting Things Done by David Allen
A seriously intense organization system. We've fallen off the wagon more times than we can count, but even if we're not GTDers anymore, David Allen's philosophy is still with us.

How to Have a Good Day by Caroline Webb
Deeper analysis of the latest behavioral science and smart recommendations for how to apply that science to your daily life.

The Power of Moments by Chip and Dan Heath
The Heath brothers explain why moments have an outsize influence on our lives, then show how you can engineer great moments in yours. Read this book and tackle your Highlights with renewed vigor.

Headspace app starring Andy Puddicombe
Andy does more than guide you through meditation—he teaches a great mindset for the modern world.

The Power of Habit by Charles Duhigg
Use this as a guide for converting Make Time tactics into long-term habits.

Mindset by Carol Dweck
Habits are very powerful, but sometimes you need a mindset shift to change your behavior.

In Defense of Food by Michael Pollan
There's no better guide to building energy by eating like a hunter-gatherer.

Sapiens by Yuval Noah Harari
Many of the Make Time tactics are based on the idea of learning from ancient humans. *Sapiens* is a detailed, remarkable history of, well . . . humans.

For a more thorough critique of the industry of distraction, check out *Irresistible* by Adam Alter, the Center for Humane Technology website by Tristan Harris (humanetech.com), and, for a look at how habit-forming products are designed, *Hooked* by Nir Eyal.

Here are a few personal suggestions from each of us:

JZ

Your Money or Your Life by Vicki Robin and Joe Dominguez
This classic book applies the same principles as Make Time—rethinking defaults, being intentional, avoiding distraction—to the topic of personal finance. It's surprisingly inspirational.

A Guide to the Good Life by William B. Irvine
A very accessible introduction to Stoic philosophy. Like Make Time, Stoicism is a daily system with tactics for living life—but it's more than 2,000 years old.

As Long as It's Fun by Herb McCormick
This is a different kind of suggestion: a biography about a couple who chose to create their own defaults, building two boats by hand, sailing twice around the world, and writing eleven books. Pure inspiration.

Jake

The Living by Annie Dillard
This novel (set near where I grew up, in northwestern Washington State) gave me an appreciation for life and moments that has stuck with me for decades.

On Writing by Stephen King
Naturally, this is a must-read for an aspiring fiction writer like myself. But you don't have to be a writer or a horror fan (I'm not) to love this book. It's packed with lessons on doing *any* work with diligence and passion. And it's hilarious.

Finally, we both agree you should read . . .

Sprint by Jake Knapp, John Zeratsky, and Braden Kowitz
If you like the ideas in *Make Time,* try a design sprint at work.

SHARE YOUR TACTICS, FIND RESOURCES, AND GET IN TOUCH

To find the latest apps to help with Make Time, read new tactics from us and other readers, and share your own techniques, please check out maketimebook.com and sign up for our newsletter.

THANK-YOU NOTES

Awesome people who helped us write this book:

Our excellent agent, Sylvie Greenberg, who took us from a pile of blog posts all the way to a finished book. And a huge thanks to our team at Fletcher & Company—Erin McFadden, Grainne Fox, Veronica Goldstein, Sarah Fuentes, Melissa Chinchillo, and of course Christy Fletcher.

Our brilliant editor, Talia Krohn, who helped us focus on what mattered and create the most useful book possible. And high fives to the entire team at Currency—Tina Constable, Campbell Wharton, Erin Little, Nicole McArdle, Megan Schumann, Craig Adams, and Andrea Lau.

Our UK editor, Andrea Henry, who delivered smart and perfectly timed feedback.

Our early readers Josh Yellin, Imola Unger, Mia Mabanta, Scott Jenson, Jonathan Courtney, Stefan Claussen, Ryan Brown, Daren Nicholson, Piper Loyd, Kristen Brillantes, Marin Licina, Bruna Silva, Stéph Cruchon, Joseph Newell, John Fitch, Manu Cornet, Boaz Gavish, Mel Destefano, Tim Hoefer, Camille Fleming, Michael Leggett, Henrik Bay, Heidi Miller, Martin Loensmann, Daniel Andefors,

Anna Andefors, Tish Knapp, Xander Pollock, Maleesa Pollock, Becky Warren, Roger Warren, Francis Cortez, Matt Storey, Sean Roach, Tin Kadoic, Cindy Fenton, Jack Russillo, Dave Cirilli, Dee Scarano, Mitchell Geere, Rebecca Garza-Bortman, Amy Bonsall, Josh Porter, Rob Hamblen, Michael Smart, Ranjan Jagganathan, and Douglas Ferguson, who gave us honest reactions and insightful suggestions. This book is much better for your efforts.

Our 1,700+ test readers, who helped us clarify and de-boring-ify the beginning of *Make Time*, and who are so numerous they get their own section with really tiny type on page 272.

JZ

First thanks go to my wife, Michelle. You're the best. Thanks for supporting this project, even when I wrote the first outline during a vacation together in St. John. Even when working on the book overlapped with our sailing plans. And especially when you read the manuscript several times, giving me smart feedback from a much-needed perspective. Thank you very much.

Thank you, Jake. As I write this, it's been six years since our first design sprint together. Working with you has changed how I think about work itself. Our collaboration isn't something I could have planned or anticipated. Most of all, it's just been really fun! Let's do it again.

Thanks to my friends who have been role models at work. To Mike Zitt, who was an early example of how to redesign work to support life. To Matt Shobe, who showed me the power of wholehearted creative work (and for being a fantastic mentor in copywriting). To Graham Jenkin, who demonstrated how even managers with full calendars can make time for what matters. And to Kristen Brillantes and Daniel Burka, who showed how amazing things can happen when you bring your whole self to work.

Thank you, Taylor Hughes, Rizwan Sattar, Brenden Mulligan, Nick Burka, and Daniel Burka for more than ten years of turning my Make Time ideas into apps. I'll always be grateful for Done-zo, Compose, and One Big Thing.

Thanks to the writers (and other influences) who have changed how I think about time, energy, and life. Especially Cal Newport, Gretchen Rubin, James Altucher, Jason Fried, JD Roth, Laura Vanderkam, Lin Pardey, Mark Sisson, Nassim Taleb, Pat Schulte, Paula Pant, Pete Adeney, Steven Pressfield, Vicki Robin, and Warren Buffett.

Jake

My biggest thanks go to my lovely wife, Holly. I wouldn't and couldn't have written this book without your steady encouragement and hard-nosed feedback (I say "hard-nosed" in the most complimentary way possible). You make me very happy, and I appreciate it.

Luke, thank you for introducing me to time management by being born. And thanks for being a steady friend throughout this long project, and for lending me your design eye.

Flynn, thank you for being fun and encouraging me to take breaks from writing. Also, thanks for working alongside me on the illustrations.

Mom, thanks for typing up my elementary school stories, putting up with my snark in twelfth-grade English, and helping me get the words right in *Make Time*. And most important, thank you for writing books and showing me such a thing was possible. If I'm a writer, it's because of you.

For many, many years, the Gandhi quote at the beginning of this book was taped to the dashboard of my dad's pickup truck. My dad lived that quote. Throughout his life, day after day, he made unconventional choices to slow down and put quality of time ahead of money or prestige. He won't get to see this book, but I had him in mind every time I sat down to write. Dad, I sure miss you—thanks for teaching me to pay attention.

Many friends have inspired me with their approach to life and time. Instead of trying to mention everyone, I'll just focus on two who especially shaped my thinking. Scott Jenson and Kristen Brillantes, you rock.

I feel lucky to have the opportunity to publish a book, and I'm grateful to the many people who helped open that door to me, among them Sylvie Greenberg, Christy Fletcher, Ben Loehnen, Tim Brown, Nir Eyal, Eric Ries, Bill Maris, Braden Kowitz, and Charles Duhigg.

This book is also a fan letter to the writers who changed how I think about my days, especially Daniel Pinkwater, David Allen, Gretchen Rubin, June Burn, Jason Fried, Barbara Kingsolver, Tim Urban, Annie Dillard, Tim Ferriss, Stephen King, Austin Kleon, Scott Berkun, Dan Ariely, Marie Kondo, Tom and David Kelley, and Chip and Dan Heath. On the off chance any of you writers are reading the acknowledgments of a self-help book right now: Consider this a coupon for a cup of coffee on me, anytime.

And of course, a super deluxe thank-you to my great friend John Zeratsky. Thanks for your enthusiasm, patience, intelligence, insight, diligence, and constructive disagreements. Your worldview has inspired me since we met, and it was a pleasure working with you—even when you up and sailed to Mexico.

ILLUSTRATION CREDITS

Illustrations by Jake Knapp

Phone and laptop wallpaper photos by Luke Knapp

Some coloring by Flynn Knapp

MAKE TIME NOTES   DATE _____

TODAY'S **HIGHLIGHT**

DID I MAKE TIME FOR IT? **YES! NO.**

TODAY'S FOCUS

LASER   (1 2 3 4 5 6 7 8 9 10)

TODAY'S ENERGY

ENERGIZE   (1 2 3 4 5 6 7 8 9 10)

TACTICS TRIED TODAY: HOW DID IT GO?

TACTICS TO TRY (OR TRY AGAIN) TOMORROW:

MOMENT I'M GRATEFUL FOR:

MAKE TIME TEST READERS

Thank you to the 1,700 readers who signed up to review an early version of this book and gave us excellent input. We hope we didn't miss anyone or misspell any names, but if we did, just know we appreciate you all the same:

Aaron Bright, MD • Aaron J. Palmer • Aaron Matys • Aaron Rosenberg • Aaron Stites • Aaron • Aarron Walter • Abdulaziz Azzahrani • Abe Crystal • Abhay Shah • Abhishek Kona • Abraham Orellanes • Ad Bresser • Adam • Adam Armstrong • Adam Brooks • Adam Egger • Adam La France • Adam Waxman • Adam Williams • Adarsh Pandit • Adithya J • Aditi Ruiz • Adler • Adrian Abele • Adriano • Adrien • Adrien Gomar • Adrienne Brown • Agha Zain • Agnese Bite • Ahmad Alim Akhsan • Ahmad Fairiz • Ahmad Nursalim • Aileen Bennett • Aina Azmi • Akash Shukla • Alan Tsen • Alan Wojciechowski • Alan Worden • Alar Kolk • Alastair Baker • Albert Ramirez Canalias • Alberto S. Rodrigues Jr. • Alberto Samaniego • Alec James van Rassel • Alejandra • Alejandra Cabrera • Alejandro G. Jack • Alejo Rivera • Alessandro Fusco • Alex Bates • Alex Drago • Alex McNeal • Alex Morris • Alex Sherman • Alex Shuck • Alex Uribe • Alexander Baumgardt • Alexander Krieger • Alexander Paluch • Alexander Zdrok • Alexandre do Amaral Ferrari • Ali Chelibane • Ali Rushdan Tariq • Alice Ralph • Alice White • Alin Tuhut • Allan Lykke Christensen • Alli Myatt •

Allison Marie Cooper • Alonso Vargas Esparza • Alvin Rentsch • Aman Mayson • Amaresh Ray • Amber Siscoe Vasquez • Amicis Arvizu • Amir Abbas • Amit Jain • Amjad Sidqi • Amjid Rasool • Amy Bonsall • Amy Bucciarelli • Amy Chan • Amy DeMoss • Amy J. Buechel • Amy Jo Kim • Amy Mitchell • Amy Parent • Amy Sanders • Ana Karina Caudillo • Ana Lucia • Ana Manrique • Ana Paula Batista • Analisa Ornelas • Anant Jain • Anastasia Gritsenko • Anders Heibrock Mortensen • Anders Wik • André Azevedo • Andre de la Cruz • Andre Nordal Sylte • Andrea Andrews • Andrea Dinneen • Andrea Pashayan • Andrea Romoli • Andrea Wong • Andreas Barhainski • Andreas Cem Vogt • Andreas Knaut • Andreea Mihalcea • Andreia • Andreia Ribeiro • Andres Calderon • Andres Villegas Mesa • Andrew Croasdale • Andrew Kong • Andrew Look • Andrew May • Andrew Peters • Andrew Willis • Andy Boydston • Andy Burnham • Andy Howard • Andy Hugelier • Andy Orsow • Andy Rose • Aneeb Ahmed • Angelica Speich • Angélica Speich • Angie Greenham • Angus Tait • Ankur Kaul • Ann MacKay • Ann Mueller • Anna Andefors • Anna Endres • Anna Iurchenko • Anne Pedro • Anne-Laure Jourdain • Annelie Weinehall • Annette • Annette Achermann • Annette Q. Pedersen • Annette Rodriguez • Annia Monroy Dugelby • Anonymous • Antal János Monori • Anthony James Amici • Antoine Nasser • Antoine Sakho • Anton Jarl • Anton Nikolov • Antonia Ciaverella • Antonio Sánchez Pineda • Antonio Starnino • Antonio Storino • Antoon Melchers • Anuj Duggal • Anurag Adhikary • April Xu • Apurva Pathak • Arb • Arie-Jan Lommers • Ario Jafarzadeh • Arjan de Jong • Arnaud Carrette • Arnaud Le Roux • Arthur Mellors • Arthur von Kriegenbergh • Artur • Artur Eldib • Artur Pokusin • Arturo Lopez Valerio • Arturo Perez Enciso • Arun Kumar • Arun Martin • Arva Adams • Ashita Achuthan • Asia Hege • Assaf Guery • Atar • Athena Zhao • Atif Raza • Axel J. Tullmann • Ayanna Haskins • Ayse McMillan • Bar Wiegman • Barbara Neves Kich • Barbara Valenti • Bart Engels • Bart Melort • Bart Tkaczyk • Bas Kok • Bastian • Bastian M. • Ben Barnett • Ben Havill • Ben Hewitt • Ben Jackson • Ben Phillips • Ben White • Benjamin Miraski • Benson Tait • Benyamin Najafi • Bernard Lindekens • Bernardo Mazzini • Bernardo Núñez Rojas • Bertus Hölscher • Betina Merrild Yde • Bhanu G. • Bharat Saini • Bill Bulman • Bill Cotter • Bill Seitz • Binusha Perera • Björn Barleben • Blair Rorani • Bliss Siman • Boaz Gavish • Bob Dohnal • Bob Monroe •

Bogdan Domu • Bohuslav Dohnal • Bosco Zubiaga • Brad Ledford • Brad Snyder • Bree Playel • Bree Thomas • Brendan Kearns • Brendan Raftery • Brenden Rodriguez • Brett Flora • Brian Alexander Lee • Brian Bajzek • Brian Burns • Brian Frank • Brian Kasen • Brian McCormack • Brian Oberkirch • Brian van Stokkum • Brooks Grigson • Bruce Bullis • Bruna Silva • Bruno Campos • Bryan Postelnek • Bryan Walters • Bryann Alexandros • Bryonie Badcock • Bülent Duagi • Buphinder Thapar • Bur Zeratsky • Byron Silver • Caitlin Hudon • Cameron Compton • Cameron Malek • Camila Rodrigues • Carien • Carlee Malkowski • Carlo Zuffa • Carlos Andres Jaramillo Abad • Carlos Baeza Vásquez • Carlos Diaz • Carlos Freitas • Carlos Mendes • Carolien Postma • Caroline Michaud • Carrie • Carrie Kim • Carrie Tian • Carrie Wiley • Cash • Casimir Morreau • Casper Klenz-Kitenge • Casper Kold • Casper Wolfert • Cathan Milton • Cathrine Fallesen • CelloJoe • César Franca • César García • Chaiyarat Soontornprapee • Chandler Roth • Charbel Semaan • Charles Reynolds-Talbot • Charles Riccardi • Charles Rice • Charles Shryock, IV • Charlie Drew • Charlie Park • Charlotte B. • Charly Mendoza • Chelsey Schaffel • Cheryl Hosking • Chiara Giovanni • Chino • Chino Wong • Chip Dong Lim • Chip Trout • Chris • Chris Alvarez • Chris Barbin • Chris Barning • Chris Bobbitt • Chris Bowler • Chris Brisson • Chris Chappelle • Chris Conover • Chris Dee • Chris Dennett • Chris Gorges • Chris Henderson • Chris Janin • Chris M. • Chris McQueen • Chris Nottle • Chris Palmieri • Chris Sanders • Chris Superfly Jackson • Chris van Leeuwen • Chris Vander Ark • Christian Andersen • Christian Beltrao Andersen • Christian Fuglsang • Christian Mueller • Christian van Leeuwen • Christina Himmelev • Christine Avesen O. Balatbat • Christine Chong • Christoffer Kittel • Christoph Faschian • Christoph Steindl • Christopher "Bibby" Howett • Christopher Lynn • Christopher Polack • Christopher Schroer • Chuangming Liu • Chuck Ward • Chunhao Weng • Ciarán Hanrahan • Cindi Ramm • Cindy Fenton • Claire Hutt • Claire Shapiro • Claudia Melo • Claudio Stivala • Claus Berthou Madsen • Clay Ostrom • Cloed Baumgartner • Colin Clark • Colin Jones • Colin Lernell • Colm Roche • Connor Swenson • Corrado Francolini • Costinel Marin • Courtney Gallagher • Courtney Tulig • Covington Doan • Craig Higton • Craig Merry • Craig Primack • Cyrille Le Rolland • Daan van de Kamp • Damian Fok • Damien Newman • Dan Aschwanden • Dan Benoni

• Dan Carroll • Dan Oxnam • Dan Shiner • Dan Weingrod • Dani Glikmanas • Daniel • Daniel Andefors • Daniel Bartel • Daniel Fosco • Daniel Jarjoura • Daniel Kašaj • Daniel Leo Buckley • Daniel Miller • Daniel N. • Daniel R. Farrell • Daniel Ronsman • Daniel Stillman • Daniel Yubi • Danikka Dillon • Danilo Toledo • Danilo Visco • Danni Hu • Danny Holtschke • Danny Spitzberg • Danny Tamez III • Daren Nicholson • Darren Anthony Taylor • Darren Brandwood • Darren Yeo • Darri Ulfsson • Darryn • Darryn Lifson • Dave Best • Dave Cirilli • Dave Hoodspiht (Hoody) • Dave Miklasevich • David Agasi • david beasley • David Breizna • David Bryan • David Buxton • David C. Weinel • David Franke • David G. Hall • David Glauber • David Holl • David Hoogland • David Jones • David McGrath • David Roche • David Rosenberg • David Thayer • David Walker • David Whipps • Dean Hudson • Deandra Hendrix • Debbie Cotton • Debora Bottà • Dede Nesbitt • Dee Scarano • Deke Bowman • Denis Bartelt • Dennis Furia • Derek Punsalan • Derek Winter • Derick Jose • Devin O'Neil • Devin Pope • Di Mayze • Diana Dragomir • Diana Padron • Diana Pottecher • Dianna Hardy • Dietmar Stefl-Sedlnitzky • Dima Koshevoi • Dimitry Galamiyev • Diogo Romeo Rosanelli • Dipika Mallya • Dirk Belling • Dirk Hens • Divyen Sanganee • Dmitry Krasnoperov • Domenico Giuseppe Nicosia • Dominik Kühner • Don Lenere Woods • Donald Vossen • Donnie Tristan Minnick • Doug Field • Doug Gould • Doug Mather • Doug Tabuchi • Douglas Ferguson • Douglas Nash • Dr. Paul Schultz • Drew Gorham • Dylan Weiss • Dynin Khem • E. Forsack • Ed • Ed Matesevac • Ed McCauley • Eddie Harran • Edmund Komar • Edmund O'Shaughnessy • Eduardo Del Torno • Eduardo H Calvillo-Gamez • Eduardo Peña • Edward Jones • Ehrik Aldana • Eirik Torheim Gilje • Elena Timofeeva • Eli Shillock • Eliot Gattegno • Elizabeth Jarrold • Elizabeth Sankey • Elizabeth Ziegler • Ella Obreja • Ellie Booth • Elmar Kruitwagen • Elodie Rival • Elsa Wormeck • Elzaan Pienaar • Emil Sotirov • Emily Campbell • Emily O'Byrne • Emily Swope Brower • Emma Linh • Emma Rosenberg • EmmanuelG • Eric Garcia • Eric Herrera • Eric J. Garcia • Eric Sinclair • Erica Bjornsson • Erica Key • Erik Arvedson • Erin • Erin Moore • Erin Pinkley • Eron Villarreal • Ethan Cleary • Eunice Sari • Eusebio Reyero • Evan Portwood • Ezequiel Aguilar • F. Marek Modzelewski • Fabian Fischer • Fabian Steiner • Fabrice Liut • Farhad Pocha • Federico Malagoli • Felipe Barbosa • Felipe Castro • Felipe Jiménez Cano

• Felipe Pontes • Femi Longe • Femmebot • Feridoon "Doon" Malekzadeh • Fernando Agüero • Fernando Arguelles • Flemming Westberg • Florian Fiechter • Florian Lissot • Florin Sirghea • Francis Cortez • Francis Peixoto • Francis Wade • Francisco Baptista • Francisco González • Francois Brill • François Luc Moraud • Frank • Frank Decavele • Frank Devitt • Frank Jablonski • Frank Pineda • Frank R. • Fred Leveau • Fredrik Johansson • Fredrik Nordell • Fri Rasyidi • Gabor Kiss • Gabor Labancz • Gabriel Garcia • Gabriela Aguirrezabal • Galit Lurya • Gar Morley • Gareth H. McShane • Gareth Kay • Garin Bulger • Garrett Sheridan • Gary Kahn • Gaspard Chameroy • Gaston Serpenti • Gaurav Bhargva • Gaurav Bhargva • Gauresh R. Khanolkar • Gautam Lakum • Gavin Esajas • Gavin Montague • Geert Claes • Geetha Pai • Gemma Curl • Gennadiy Nissenbaum • Geoff Cardillo • Geoffrey Gentry • Geoffrey Lew • George Jigalin • Gerald Carvalho • Ghalib Hussaiyn • Gianfranco Palumbo • Gideon Bullock • Gideon Hornung • Gil Shklarski • Giles Peyton-Nicoll • Gillian • Gillian Julius • Giorgio Pauletto • Giorgos Gavriil • Giovani Ferreira • Giovanni Caruso • Giovanni Dal Sasso • Gitta Salomon • Glen Crosier • Glenn Exton • Glenna Baron • Gordon Soutar • Gostandinos Christofi • Graeme Wheatley • Graham North • Grandin Donovan • Greg • Greg Bennett • Greg Dudish • Greg Palmer • Gregg Bernstein • Gregg Mayer • Gregory Milani • Gregory Thompson • Guido van Glabbeek • Gustavo del Valle • Gustavo Gawryszewski • Gustavo Machado • Gustavo Reyes • Guy Dickinson • Guy Van Wijmeersch • Halina Mugame • Hameed Haqparwar • Hana Kim • Hang-Tien Lin • Hari Narasimhan • Hassan Syed • Haya Alzaid • Heath Sadlier • Heather Guith • Heather Pettrey • Héctor Calleja • Hector Cardenas • Hedd Roberts • Heidi Miller • Heidi Shipp • Helen • Helen King • Helene Desliens • Hendrik Will • Hendry Sumilo • Hennadiy Kornev • Henrik Bay • Henrik Mitsch • Henrique L. Ribeiro • Henry Soo • Hera Kan • herrK • Hesam Panahi • Holly May Mahoney • Hongyuan Jiang • Horia Sas • Howard Barrett • Hugh Knowles • Hung Le • Hunter Walk • Hwang Seulchan • Hye young Kim (Khaily Kim) • Iaco Berra • Ibraheem Khalifa • Ievgen Ishchuk • Ilhan Scheer • Imola Unger • Imran • Imran Ur-Rehman • Inês Santos Silva • Ingunn Aursnes • Ira Weiss • Irene Meister • Irsan Widarto • Irv Bartlett • Isaac Girard • Ismail Ali Manik • István Kuti • Istvan Nagy-Racz • Ivan Molto • Ivan Zaichuk • Ivana Lukes Rybanska • Ivar Lyngve • Ivo van Hurne • J. Tristram

• Jaakko Palokangas • Jack Russillo • Jackson B. • Jacob Colling • Jacob Hage • Jacob McDonald • Jaime Moncada • Jake Colling • Jake Kendall • Jameel Sadruddin Somji • James Carleton • James Lewis • James Lutley • James McDonough • James McGary • James OConnor • James Saunders • James Tao • James Willeford • Jamie Ambler • Jamie Treyvaud • Jamison Shelton • Jan Andersson • Jan Antonin Kolar • Jan Korsanke • Jan Rosa • Jan Seversson • Jared Volpe • Jarryd Hennequin • Jason Carolan • Jason Cooke • Jason Crane • Jason Danyluk • Jason Grant • Jason Horne • Jason M. Banks • Jason Ralls • Jason Rodriguez • Jason Roe • Jason Thorarinsson • Jaspar Roos • Jasper Huang • Jasper Lyons • Jay Eskenazi • Jay OHare • Jay Thrash • Jayne Nguyen • Jeanette Cajide • Jed Brown • Jed Said • Jeevan Jayaprakash • Jeff Blanchard • Jeff Corkran • Jeff McGrath • Jeff Melton • Jeffrey Lin • Jeffrey Mack • Jeffrey Veen • Jena Donlin • Jenifer Padilla • Jenna Dixon • Jennifer Abella • Jennifer Arzt • Jennifer Conant • Jennifer Schuchmann • Jenniffer Whittingham • Jenny Fürstenbach • Jenny Massey • Jeppe Lambæk • Jered Odegard • Jeremy Caplan • Jeroen Goddijn • Jeroen Razoux Schultz • Jeroen van Beek • Jerry Borunda Junior • Jess Telford • Jesse Brack • Jesse Forest • Jessica L. Williams • Jessica Turner • Jet van Genuchten • Jiani Li • Jill Harmon • Jim Evers • Jim McDonough • Jim Peluso • Jimi Lee Friis • Jimmy Coleman • Jing Zhang • JJ MacLean • JJ Soracco • JLink • Joacim Alm • Joanne Magbitang • Joe Alicata • Joe Barbuto • Joe Moran • Joel Davis • Joelene Weeks • Joh Tienks • John Behrens • John C. Malley • John Cassidy • John Cleere • John Cockrell • John Daniel McGinnis • John Ferrigan • John Fitch • John Gusiff • John Hodgins • John Kembel • John L. Warren • John Loftus • John McGinnis • John Phippen • John Shoffner • John Tristram • John Williams Taylor • John Zimmerman • Jon Gold • Jon Hoover • Jon Izquierdo • Jon-Allan Pearson • Jonathan • Jonathan Caldwell • Jonathan Courtney • Jonathan DeFaveri • Jonathan Diehl • Jonathan Drake • Jonathan Lo • Jonathan McCoubrey • Jonathan Minchin • Jonathan R. Drake • Jonathan Rogers • Jonathan Simcoe • Joost van Schie • Jordan Carr • Jordan Robinson • Jorge Sanchez • Jorunn D. Newth • Jose Platero • Joseph Newell • Josh Kasten • Josh Kubicki • Josh Porter • Josh Turk • Josh Yellin • Joshua Anderton • Joshua Boggs • Joshua Dance • Joshua Galan • Joshua Marshall • Joshua Morris • Joshua Nafman • Josie • Josue B. Garnica • Juan Lombana • Juan Manuel Pasten Martinez • Juan Milleiro • Juan Orozco • Juan Pao • Juergen

Koehler • Juleigh Pisciotti • Julia • Julia Butter • Julia Caruso • Julian Austin • Juliana Morozowski • Julianna Probst • Julie Harris • Julien Legat • Juliet Kaplan • Juliette Hauville • Julio Gomez • Jun Hongo • Justin Calingasan • Justin Copeland • Justin Davis • Justin Mathew • Justin Schafer • Justin Swedberg • Justin Talmadge • Justine Win Canete • K. S. S. Raj • Kait Gaiss • Kal Gangavarapu • Karen • Karen Lovejoy • Karen McDonald • Karen Scruggs • Karin Kiesl • Karis Dorrigan • Karl Adriansson • Karsten Mikaelsen • Karsten Nebe • Karsten Ploesser • Kash • Kash Baghaei • Kat Palmer • Kate Flynn • Katharina Simon • Kathy Davies • Kathy Sirui Liu • Kati Tawast • Katie B. London • Katie Dehler • Katie Glass • Katie Moss • Katie Priest • Katrine • Kayode Dada • KC • K.C. Oh • Keerthi Surapaneni • Keith Grinsted • Keith Hopper • Keledy Kenkel • Kellie White • Kelly Larbes • Kelo Kubu • Kelvin O'Shea • Ken Louise • Ken Randall • Kenji Natsumoto • Kennedy Kahiri • Kennith Leung • Kenny Chen • Kevin Bachus • Kevin Blemel • Kevin Fidelin • Kevin Flores • Kevin Henry • Kevin Lücke • Kevin M. Jackson • Khaled Wagdy • Khemya • Khor Zijian • Kim Aage Ditlefsen • Kim Hurtado • Kimitoshi Saji • Kiran Kumar Nagaraj • Kirsten • Kirsten Disse • Kit • Knut-Jørgen Rishaug • Koraldo Kajanaku • Kota Okazaki • Kristen Brillantes • Kristen Rutherford • Kristian Manrique • Kristina Cunningham Bigler • Kristina Lins • Kristoffer • Kristoffer Stenseth • Kristoffer Tjalve • Krzysztof Przybylski • Kuba Butkowski • Kunal Punjabi • Kursat Ozenc • Kyle McEnery • Kyle Nash • Landon C. Akiyama • Lars Olof Berg • Larysa Visengeriyeva • Laura K Spencer, Ed.D • Laura Thompson • Lauren M. Fischer • Lavrenti Tsudakov • le Rolland • Leah • Leandro Gama • Lee Delgado • Lee Duncan • Lee Jun Lin • Lee Smith • Len Yeh • Leo Almeida • Léo Cabral • Leo Tolstoy • Levi Brooks • Lewis Kang'ethe Ngugi • Lewis Ngugi • Lianne Siemensma • Libor Vanc • Lillian Courtney • Lillian Courtney Coaching • Lina Praškevičiūtė • Lisa Gay Bostwick • Lisa Kurz • Lisa Tjide • Lisa van Mastbergen • Liviu Sirghea • Liz Eden • Liz Lee • Lizzie • Lizzie Weiland • Logan Leger • Loida Valentin • Lorelei Munroe • Lorenzo Hodges • Lorraine Marsh • Lotte Lund Larsen • Lou Fox • Louise W. Klinker • Luca Troisi • Lucas Baraças • Lucas Baraças Figueiredo • Lucas Rowe • Lucas Seidenfaden • Lucile Foroni • Luis Borges • Luis Delgado • Luis R. Meza • Luis Roberto Brenes • Luis X. González • Lukas Arvidsson • Lukas Imrich • Lukas Klinser • Lukas Misko • Łukasz Tyrała • Luke Brooker •

Luke Summerfield • Luther C. Lotz II • Luuk van Hees • Lydia Henshaw • Maanavi Tandan • Maciej Gawlik • Madison Spangler • Mads Hensel • Magdalena Małachowska • Maggie Gram • Maggie Powers • Magnus Askenbäck • Magrafx • Maia Sciupac • Maicol Parker-Chavez • Maja Kathrine Lundholm Larsen • Majbritt Sandberg • Maks Majer • Mal Piernik • Maleesa Pollock • Małgorzata Piernik • Manchi Chung • Manny • Manu Cornet • Manuel • Manuel Vigo • Manuele Capacci • Marc Anthony Rosa • Marc Augustin • Marc Emil Domar • Marc Sirkin • Marc Snyder • Marc-Oliver Gern • Marcella Borasque de Paula • Marcelo Paiva • Marcelo Quinta • MarcelR • Marciano Planque • Marco Lohnes • Marco Pardini • Marco Poli • Marcos Ortiz • Marcus Carr • Marcy Chu • Marek Gebka • Marek Modzelewski • Margaret Powers • Margriet Buseman • María Fernanda Flores • María Fernanda Flores G. • María Gracia Morales • Maria Haynie • Maria M. Fabbroni • Marie-Blanche Panthou • Marie-Haude Meriguet • Mariela Barzallo León • Marin Licina • Mario Alberto Galindo • Mario Duck • Mario Galindo • Mario Gamboa-Cavazos • Mario López De Ávila Muñoz • Marion Neumann • Maritta • Mark A. Hart • Mark Arteaga • Mark Bucherl • Mark Bucknell • Mark Butler • Mark Cook • Mark Downey • Mark Garner • Mark Macfarlane • Mark Smith • Mark Stevens • Mark Swaine • Mark Winsper • Mark Zhou • Marko Dugonjić • Marko Soikkeli • Markus "Marek" Gebka • Markus Huehn • Mart Maasik • Martha Valenta • Martin Carty • Martin Hoffmann • Martin Huijbregts • Martin Kerr • Martin Konrad Gloeckle • Martin Kremmer • Martin Labrousse • Martin Loensmann • Martin Nathan • Martin P. Sötzen • Martin Tangel • Martin Veldsman • Martin Wiman • Marv Gillibrand • Mary Selby • Mateus Barreto • Mateusz Tylicki • Matias Bejas • Mats Hansson • Matt Bjornson • Matt Dobson • Matt Dominici • Matt Harbord • Matt Koidin • Matt Martin • Matt Robbins • Matt Storey • Matt Zuerrer • Matte Scheinker • Matteo Roversi • Matthew Borenstein • Matthew Cunningham • Matthew Hawn • Matthew Lee • Matthew Moran • Matthew Robbins • Maureen Macharia • Mauricio Angulo S. • Mauricio Martinez • Max Birbes • Max La Rivière-Hedrick • Max Pekarsky • Max Stanworth • Maxim Pekarsky • May Thawdar Oo • May Woo • Megann Willson • Meghan Nesta • Meirion Mez Williams • Mel Destefano • Melanie Kahl • Melina Pierro • Melissa Beaver • Melissa Collier • Melissa Flores • Melissa Lacitignola • Melissa Lang • Melissa McCollum • Memo Muñoz

Urbina • Mia Mabanta • Michael Beach • Michael Braasch • Michael Bracklo • Michael Davidson • Michael Facchinello • Michael Farley • Michael Harris • Michael Jones • Michael Leggett • Michael Neff • Michael Nikitochkin • Michael Pavey • Michael Sartor • Michael Sitver • Michael Smart • Michael Stencl • Michael Wickett • Michal Nalepka • Michel Jansen • Michell Geere • Michelle Brien • Michelle Dunford-Elliott • Michelle Swan • Mideum Lee • Miguel Vazquez • Mika Jovicic • Mike Barker • Mike Brand • Mike Carpenter • Mike Caskey • Mike Herrmann • Mike Leber • Mike Lovas • Mike Mirabella • Mike Moss • Mike Tobias • Mike Williams • Millie • Misty Karen Antatico • Mitchell Smith • Mitushi Jain • Mo • Moe Abdou • Mogens Skjold • Mohammed Pitolwala • Mohammed Sahli • Mohan Nadarajah • Mollie Duffy • Molly Stevens • Mona Hakky • Monte K. Youngs • MoraMorais • Morgan Lindsay • Morgan Sheeran • Morten Hannibalsen Olsen • Mrinalini Kamath • M.T. Williams • Mudassir Azeemi • Munir Ahmad • Myles • Nadine Steinacker • Nandha • Nandhagopal • Nandini • Nandini Bhardwaj • Natalie Bomberry • Natalie Hewton-Waters • Nate Osborne • Nate W. Godfrey • Nathalia Albar • Nathan Llewellyn • Nathan Wunsch • Nathanael Smith • Naz Hamid • Nealle Page • Neeraj Hirani • Neha Saigal • Nelson Canro • Nenad • Nenad Jelovac • Nicholas Evans • Nick Burka • Nick Busscher • Nick Casares • Nick Chronis • Nick Hallam • Nick Harewood • Nick John Lopez Villaverde • Nick Karpetis • Nick Ng • Nick Ruzhnikov • Nick Sherrard • Nick Stevens • Nick White • Nickolaus Casares • Nicky • Nicky Godden • Nicola De Filippo • Nicolai Fogh • Nicolás Alliaume • Nicolas Hemidy • Nicole Landry • Niels Bruin • Nigel Quinlan • Nikhileswar Jangala • Nikki Will • Nils Smed • Nima Bousejin • Nima Roohi Sefidmazgi • Nina Kostamo Deschamps • Nina Wilken • Nir Eyal • Niraj Shekhar • Nish • Nishant Bhalla • Nitya Narasimhan • Nobuya Sato • Noel Keener • Noel Peden • Norman Tran • Nuno Coelho Santos • Oday mashalla • Ole Rich Henningsen • Olga Repnikova • Oliver Vassard • Olufemi Olowolafe II • Omar B. Sanduka • Omar Rodríguez Bermello • Omid Elliyoun • Oon Arfiandwi • Oscar Aguayo • Oscar Heed • Owen McCrink • Oz Lubling • Paolo Rovelli • Paolo Tripodi • Paris H. • Parita Kapadia • Parveen Kaler • Pascal Michelet • Patrici Flores • Patrick Barrett • Patrick DiMichele • Patrick Ehrlund • Patrick Hawley • Patrick Hodgdon • Patrick Mooney • Patrick Olszowski • Patrick Vanbrabandt • Patrick Vilain • Patti Hixon

• Paul Essene • Paul Moran • Paul Muston • Paul Nikitochkin • Paul Pilling • Paul Reijnierse • Paul Repin • Paul Strzelecki • Paul Sturrock • Pauline Thomas • Pavan S. Kanwar • Pavlo Khud • Pedro Albuquerque • Pedro José Ruíz Díaz • Pedro Ruíz • Peter Anthony Jackson • Peter D. Gilbert • Peter Goody • Peter Light • Peter Pries • Peter Slavish • Petr Stedry • Petra • Petronela Sandulache • Phil Brown • Phil Rivard • Philip Borgnes • Philip Keller • Philipp Gaul • Phyllis Treige • Pierce Smith • Pierre de Fleuriot • Pierre-Denis Autric • Piotr • Piotr Menclewicz • Piper Loyd • Prajwal M. • Pramod Nair • Prashanthi Ravanavarapu • Prateek Vasisht • Priscilla Han • Priscilla Mok • Príya Premkumar • R. Ragavendra Prasath • Rachel B. • Rachel Ilan Simpson • Rachel Lesniak • Rachmat Arsyadi • Rafael "r9rafael" Rocha • Rafael E. Landaeta, Ph.D. • Rafael Milani Archangelo • Rafał Jasiński • Rafał Kowalczyk • Raffaele Antonucci • Rafi Finegold • Rahim Ghassemi • Rahul Kapoor • Raisa Reyes • Rajan • Rajesh • Rajesh 99Aha! • Rajesh Abhyankar • Rajesh Balasubramanian • Rajesh Bhardwaj • Rajesh Viswanathan • Ralph Schmidhalter • Rama Cha • Ramesh Balakrishna • Ramon Schreuder • Ramy Nagy • Ramya • Randall Smith • Ranjan Jagannathan • Raomal Perera • Ray Campbell Lupton • Ray Tilkens • Raymond • Raymond Zhu • Rebecca Garza-Bortman • Rebecca Swan • Reg Tait • Reginald Curtis • Remo Arni • Rene Tomova • Reuben Halper • Rhys Fowler • Riad Lemhachheche • Ric Evans • Ricardo Imbert • Riccardo • Riccardo E. Giorato • Richard • Richard Bostam • Richard Pannell • Richard Phillips • Richard Shenton • Richard Thygeson Bostam • Richard Vahrman • Richard Zuber • Rick Blackwood • Rick Boersma • Rick Hennessey • Riomar Mccartney • Rish Singh • Riza Selcuk Saydam • Rob • Rob Clifton • Rob Hall • Rob Hamblen • Rob Hinckley • Rob McCoy • Robert Dale • Robert Gibson • Robert Rafiński • Robert Skrobe • Robert Wemyss • Robert Westerhuis • Robin C. • Robin Dhanwani • Robin Kraft • Rocky Gonzales • Rodrigo Estevam • Rodrigo Hurtado • Roger Navarro • Rohan Perera • Rohit • Rohit Sharma • Ron Grass • Ron Joy • Rosana Johnson • Rosemarie Withee • Ross Slater • Roy Abbink • Roz Duffy • Rudolf T. A. Greger • Rui Gomes • Ruohan • Ruohan Chen • Russell Morton • Ruzanna Rozman • Ryan • Ryan Brown • Ryan McCollum • Ryan McCutcheon • Ryan Winzenburg • S. Rao • Sabrina Vigil • Sai Krishna Rallabandi • Salva Ferrando • Sam Epstein • Sam Peckham • Samuel Hamner • Samuel J. Tanner • Sana Mohammed • Sandra

Sobanska • Sandro Pugliese • Sanjeev Arora • Santhosh Guru • Santiago Eastman • Santiago Marcó • Saoirse Charis-Graves • Sara Thurman • Sarah Cooper • Sarah Dean • Sarah Decaria • Sarah Dyer • Sarah E. Jewell • Sarah Halliday • Sarah Mondol • Sarah Revell • Sarah-Anne Alman • Saskia Clauss • Saul • Saul Diez-Guerra • Scot Westwater • Scott Hurff • Scott Jenson • Scott Shirbin • Seamus Nally • Sean Gallivan • Sean O'Connor • Sean O'Leary • Sean Roach • Sean Seungwan Lim • Sean Smith • Sean Taylor • Sebastian Koss • Sebastian Vetter • Sebastian Weise • Sébastien Faure • Seijen Takamura • Sergio • Sergio Panagia • Serguei Orozco • Shachaf Rodberg • Shane Feltham • Shane Ryan • Shanin • Shannon K'doah Range • Shari Harrison • Sharon Hsiao • Sharon Sciammas • Shau-Chau You • Shaun Adams • Shaunacy Ferro • Shawn Jones • Shefali Netke • Sheila Bulthuis • Sheldon Schwartz • Shin Lim • Shing Huei • Shirley Bunger • Shodeinde Peter Oladimeji • Shruthi Bhuma • Sid Bhargava • Signe Skriver • Silvio Gulizia • Similla Aslaksen • Simo Hakkarainen • Simon Gale • Simon H. • Simon Matty • Simon Smith • Simon Tyrrell • Simone Ellis • Simone Saldanha • Simran Thadani • Simunza Muyangana • Siri Tejani • Siva Sundaram • Siyu Chen • Slavik Kaushan • Soo Beng • Sophia Hafyane • Sophie Hwang • Søren Martin Mark Andersen • Spencer ODell • Srinivasa Kalidindi • Stefan Claussen • Stefan Petzov • Stefan Schreiber • Stefan Sohnchen • Stefanie Nagel • Steffen Meyer • Stéph Cruchon • Steph Fastre • Steph Moccia • Stephan Hammes • Stephan Kardos • Stephen Sherwin • Stephen Tomlinson • Steve Neiderhauser • Steven Mak • Steven Nguyen • Steven Twigge • Steven Villarino • Stewart Sear • Stewart Walker • Stowe Boyd • Stu Malcolm • Stuart Lawder • Sudarshana Sampath • Sudhakar Kuchibotla • Sumant Subrahmanya • Sumit Parab • Sunita Ramnarinesingh • Suprasanna Mishra • Suranga Nanayakkara • Surendra Chaplot • Surya Vanka • Susan O'Malley • Sven Lenaerts • Swaminathan Jayaraman • Swathi Bhuma • T. J. Chmielewski • Takuo Doi • Tamara • Tan Yeong Sheng • Tatiana Teixeira • Tav Klitgaard • Tawney Hughes • Taylor Wimberly • Teodor N. Rotaru • Thai Huynh • TheRealPVB • Theron D. Makley • Thiago Carvalho • Thiago Mazarão Maltempi • Thijs Loggen • Thomas Dittmer • Thomas Evans • Thomas Grill • Thomas Klein Middelink • Thomas Klueppel • Thomas Papke • Thomas Rademakers • Thomas van der Woude • Thomas William Evans • Thu Pystynen • Tiffany Zhong • Till • Till Köhler • Tim • Tim Casasola • Tim Gouw

• Tim Hoefer • Tim Schulze • Tim Upchurch • Timothy Nice • Tin Kadoic • Tish Knapp • Tobias Theil • Tobin Schwaiger-Hastanan • Toby • Todd Chambers • Tom • Tom Berkemeier • Tom Britton • Tom Cannon • Tom Hall • Tom Kane • Tom Kerwin • Tom Rantala • Tomás Nogueira • Tomasz Mirowski • Tomasz Rybak • Tomasz Szer • Tommi Ranta • Toms Rīts • Ton van der Linden • Toni Karttunen • Tony Threatt • Torry Colichio • Tosin Lanipekun • Townes Maxwell • Tracy Makkoo • Tracy Stevens • Travis B. Mitchell • Travis DeMeester • Travis Williams • Tridip Thrizu • Tristan Legros • Troels Overvad • Troy Winfrey • Trudy Cherok • Tulsi Dharmarajan • Tuomas Saarela • Tupijara • Tyler Hartrich • Tyler Leppek • Tyler McIntyre • Uma Sundaram • Ursula Pritz • Vadym Zhernovoi • Valerie Kalantyrski • Vance Stahl • Vani Henderson • Vasyl Slobodian • Vegard Jormeland • Vicki Tan • Victor Baroli • Victor M. Gonzalez • Victoria Hobbs • Victoria Schiffman • Vidhi Gyani • Vik Chadha • Vik Highland • Vikram Tiwari • Viktor Soullier • Vilav Bhatt • Viljar Rystad • Vince Law • Vincent Dromer • Virgil Cameron • Virginia J. Barnett • Vivian Agura • Vivian Gomes • Vlad Lakčević • Wagner Lucio • Warren Springer • Wayne Strong • Wesley Noah • Whui-Mei Yeo • Will Chambers • Will Dages • Will Munce • Will Vaughan • William Frazier • William Gruintal • William LaRue • William Newton • William Quezada • William Ukoh • William Wells • Willmar A. Pimentel • Wolo • Xander Pollock • Xian • Xiaojie Zheng • Xin-Fang Wu • Yashu Mittal • Yasith Abeynayaka • Yausshi Sakurai • Yohsuke Miki • Yoshinobu • Young Jang • Younghwan Cheon • Yugene • Yukiko Matsuoka • Yukio Ando • Yvonne Saidler • Zhuoshi Xie • Ziad Wakim • Zike • Zoe Moulson • Zoe T. Do • Zvi Goldfarb

INDEX

Highlight, making time for (*cont.*)
  quitting when done, 75–76
  saying no, 64–66
  scheduling Highlight, 59–60

inbox, 125–136
  about: overview of, 127–128
  dealing with at end of day, 128
  emptying weekly, 129
  locking yourself out of, 135–136
  pretending messages are letters, 129
  resetting expectations, 131–132
  responding slowly, 130–131
  scheduling time for, 128
  setting up send-only email, 132–133
  vacation without, 134
Infinity Pools
  as default with Busy Bandwagon, 4–7
  definition and reality of, 4
  difficulty resisting, 84–87
Infinity Pools, staying out of, 105–123
  avoiding time craters, 117–118
  being fair-weather sports fan, 122–123
  blocking distraction Kryptonite, 108–109
  flying without Wi-Fi, 113–114
  ignoring the news, 110–111
  putting timer on Internet, 114–116
  putting toys away, 112–113
  skipping morning check-in, 107
  trading fake wins for real, 119
  turning distractions into tools, 119–121
Internet. *See also* inbox; Infinity Pools
  cancelling, 117
  flying without Wi-Fi, 113–114
  timer on, 114–116
iPhone, 8–13, 80, 95–97, 132–133

Kryptonite, distraction, 108–109

Laser mode. *See also* distractions
  about: definition and overview, 21, 79; Make Time steps overview, 19–20
  finding, 21
  tactics. *See* email; flow, finding; inbox; Infinity Pools, staying out of; phone; TV tactics; zone, staying in

Make Time. *See also* Energize; Highlight; Laser mode; Reflect
  about: overview of, 19–20
  backstory, 14–15
  definition and objectives, 3
  "everyday mindset," 25–26
  as framework, 3
  how it works, 19–26
  no perfection required, 24–25
  "quick start" guide, 253
  tactics approach, 23–24
meditation, 213–216
Might-Do List, 50–51
morning person, becoming, 69–73
music, 149–150

napping, 204–205, 232–233
news, ignoring, 110–111, 140
notes, taking, tracking results, 241–244

paper, using instead of software, 154
perfection, 24–25
phone. *See also* Infinity Pools, staying out of
  being boss of, 91–103
  clearing homescreen, 100–101
  device-free days, 103.
    See also going off the grid
  distraction-free, 8–13, 93–97
  logging out, 98
  never stopping, 2

Start each day by
choosing a focal point

Beat distraction
to make time for
your Highlight

HIGHLIGHT > LASER > REF

ENERGIZE